Every Child Can Read

STRATEGIES AND GUIDELINES FOR HELPING STRUGGLING READERS

by Jane Baskwill and Paulette Whitman

SCHOLASTIC
PROFESSIONAL BOOKS

NEW YORK • TORONTO • LONDON • AUCKLAND • SYDNEY

Interior design by Kathy Massaro
Cover design by Laurel Marx
Cover photograph by Donnelly Marks
Interior illustrations by David Diaz

ISBN: 0-590-10389-X

Contents

Introduction

This book offers a framework called Learner Support to help you identify and support children who need extra help in their reading development. Because we are teachers ourselves, these strategies and guidelines are classroom tested; we know that they are effective and practical. Like teachers everywhere, we strive to meet the needs of the individual children who need help. At the same time, we attempt to develop supportive environments that provide appropriate learning experiences for the classroom community as a whole.

About Our Classrooms

In our classrooms, we are active participants in the learning process. We are learners as well as teachers, taking part in all that goes on. We contribute ideas, make suggestions, ask questions, share our writing, pose hypotheses, and take part in classroom activities. We are readers and writers along with the children, and we provide support and encouragement to them. By sharing some of our own successes and failures, our interests and concerns, we are better able to understand not only the children's learning processes but our own as well.

In all of this, we serve as important mentors for our students. But we are not their only models; the children also serve as models for one another. All children have particular areas of expertise, and we attempt to establish an environment in which they can share what they know with the rest of the group.

Our classrooms are often made up of mixed-age groups. We enjoy this multigrade "family" grouping because it guarantees a variety of responses from children at many levels. The children gain new perspectives and ideas from each other while feeling sufficiently assured to participate at their own level. Feeling at ease in a group situation is an important aspect of a child's developing self-esteem. We work to ensure that the children are free from the fear of making mistakes. Thus they become eager to take an active part in our learning community.

Our classroom community is also like a family because every member not only shares the responsibilities and workload but also benefits from group participation. Educator and writer Don Holdaway talks about the "communal activities" that draw the children in such a classroom together and provide them with the models and patterns they need to become independent learners. We believe that children must feel the same support and encouragement in our classrooms that they experience in their homes.

A Philosophy to Build From

Educators and researchers have discovered much about how early readers learn by looking at examples of natural learning. Early readers — those who learn to read naturally at home or who read easily upon entering school — learn to read in much the same way as they learn to speak. Adults encourage these young readers with constant support and interaction, allowing children to develop at their own rate. For most, the bedtime story is a daily ritual, a time when adult and child come together to share a book.

These children are read to repeatedly and encouraged to participate in the reading of a story, to join in whenever they feel comfortable, to ask questions, and to make connections. In this sense, the children learn to become risk-takers, to take an "educated guess" at the text.

As they observe the important people in their lives engaging in reading and writing activities, these children also learn that literacy has value. So they practice the same reading and writing behaviors independently for their own satisfaction (Doake, 1988).

In *The Foundations of Literacy*, Don Holdaway talks about incorporating the conditions necessary for natural learning into the classroom, and then provides a model for doing it. His model involves establishing a classroom as a safe, comfortable place to work and learn — a place where risk-taking is encouraged, and approximations are seen as valuable elements of the learning process.

Over the years, Holdaway's book has meant a lot to us. It serves as a reference point for our thinking about the philosophy and theory of natural learning and how we can use it to provide the best possible learning situations for children. As our Learner Support project has gained momentum, it is clear that Holdaway's model has particularly influenced the development of our classroom-based reading intervention program. And in the process, we have become better observers of what children are able to do. We have become better listeners, questioners, and conversationalists. We have also gained a great deal of personal and professional gratification from watching our classrooms develop into environments in keeping with our beliefs about children and learning.

CHAPTER 1

An Overview Of Learner Support

In today's classrooms, children are immersed in language in all its forms. They read it on the wall, the floor, and the ceiling, on labels, charts, and murals, in books and letters. They hear it as they hear stories at listening stations, as they talk and listen to one another, as they read aloud with older students, as they question and discuss with teachers and parents. They recite it to themselves. They practice new vocabulary within different contexts and, in so doing, make the language their own. They are immersed in a supportive environment where literacy behaviors are encouraged and valued, and where they are urged to take personal, individual control of their reading and writing processes.

And yet, there are often times in a child's life when learning does not go smoothly. Many children begin school with little exposure to strong literacy models at home or to books, stories, or other kinds of print. Events in family life may spill over into the school experience. And even in the most supportive learning environment, some learners may go a little "off course," or get "stuck" at a particular stage of development.

We all know these children: The ones who need more, the ones who are not progressing as well as we would hope, the ones for whom learning to read and write is a struggle despite our best efforts. They are the children we lose sleep over, who come to mind at every in-service. They are the children who, despite sound pedagogy, challenge our expertise.

Sometimes these children fall into a category labelled "at risk" because of their performance in the classroom and on diagnostic tests. Sometimes they obtain help from specialized teachers and programs, often receiving remedial assistance or "intervention" based on a pull-out model.

In recent years, the highly publicized successes of intervention programs have caused teachers to wonder whether such programs would work with particular learners in their classes. This question often leads to others: What if such intervention programs are not available locally? What if the school or district has no money to fund the training necessary to implement such programs? What about the older children who don't qualify for early intervention schemes?

These kinds of questions led to the development of the framework we call Learner Support. In essence, Learner Support is designed to help children who need extra support. Learner Support is a workable method that enables classroom teachers to help those children who, for whatever reason, do not see themselves as readers and who, therefore, are having difficulty with their reading.

Goals

The most important aim is to help all children see themselves as effective readers who *can* become independent readers. A further goal is to help children develop the ability to use reading strategies independently in a balanced and integrated manner. This involves teaching them the strategies that are appropriate for particular purposes, along with ways to monitor and regulate themselves as they read. With time and practice, the act of making a conscious decision to use a specific strategy in a given context becomes more automatic. Learner Support aims to nudge the child toward making such choices naturally.

To encourage risk-taking, Learner Support fosters self-esteem. It provides the assurance that "those around [the child] trust and support [the child's] attempts to gain personal control of what he [or she] is doing" (Holdaway, 1979, page 184). In other words, Learner Support is based on the premise that with teacher support and encouragement, children who are experiencing difficulties with their learning will gain — or regain — confidence in their abilities.

Learner Support also emphasizes that classroom experiences and special support can be integrated; it is the classroom teacher who can and should make the difference for all children.

One classroom teacher says:

"I began to feel guilty every time I referred a child to the resource teacher. I knew she didn't have any more time, but I knew that a particular child just wasn't progressing the way he should. I felt awful because I knew he needed the help. I felt that if I could just give him an extra ten or fifteen minutes here and there, I would see a difference. But I just couldn't see how to structure my day so that could happen.

Since Learner Support has come in, and we've found a way to organize those fifteen minutes into the schedule on a regular basis, I see a difference in children who are getting the extra support, and I feel good about what I'm doing."

Underlying Principles

Learner Support derives from a set of beliefs that influence how we work with children, how we plan for their learning, and how we assess and evaluate their progress.

1. *Children learn best in a safe, supportive environment that encourages risk-taking.*

Learning can be a risky business. It requires trial and error, dedication and determination. For children who are struggling, a compassionate classroom environment is crucial. Learner Support attempts to bring natural support and encouragement to one-on-one coaching, offering help on the one hand while fostering independence on the other.

2. Children learn best by doing.

Learning is an active process. Teachers recognize that it is not sufficient to tell children how to do things, or to have them master isolated skills. Instead, they help children become aware of their own strengths and needs and to monitor their own learning in real situations. In that way, children become comfortable with making personal choices in the use of appropriate strategies.

3. Children learn best when they can establish their own purposes for learning.

Learning must be authentic and purposeful, meeting genuine needs in the children's own lives. Most children want to learn to read, and those who are experiencing difficulty are usually well aware of the difference between their abilities and those of other children. Learner Support helps them to see that reading is something they too can do. It provides both a rationale as well as a support for their learning.

4. Children learn best when they are immersed in a language-rich environment that invites interaction.

Learner Support focuses on the reading aspect of literacy development, but because it is the classroom teacher who is offering it, and because the sessions are designed to take place within the classroom, there is a natural link between what goes on in the sessions and what goes on in the regular curriculum. The extra assistance children get becomes just one more element of their rich classroom experience.

5. Children learn best when the people around them demonstrate a love of learning.

Children need the chance to talk about books and reading in meaningful discussions. The interaction between teacher and child reflects what happens when two readers come together to experience the pleasure reading can bring. The teacher not only provides guidance in learning to read but also serves as the model of a lifelong reader who wants to share background experience and knowledge with a fellow reader, although a less experienced one. This relationship can be an important factor in the child's developing perception that he or she is a reader.

6. *Children learn best when they have uninterrupted blocks of time in which to learn.*

Learning takes time and children need time to become better readers. Because the reading problems children experience are varied, and because they learn and develop at their own pace and in their own way, Learner Support does not set time limits on children's involvement in the program. Some may require extra support for only a few weeks; others may need help that extends over a period of years. Learner Support provides whatever extra assistance and time is necessary.

7. *Children learn best when language is kept meaningful and whole.*

Learning does not happen in isolation. Learning — whether it is an insignificant fact or a complete procedure — is far easier when it is connected to something we already know. Teachers must use all the means at their disposal to enable children to learn the strategies they need to become better readers.

8. *Children's learning is individual. Each child learns different things at different rates and in different ways, while gradually moving along a learning continuum.*

Because learning builds on learning, teachers lead and guide by building on what the children can already do. Thus, new concepts, strategies, and techniques are introduced at the pace that is most appropriate for those children, who are then able to move forward without failure. The trusting relationship that develops between teacher and child, and the private nature of the interactions between them, provide a fail-safe learning environment in which the children can practice and experiment confidently while developing a repertoire of learning strategies to use independently.

The Role of the Teacher

Learner Support has a positive effect on teachers' learning as well as children's. It focuses not only on helping children learn to read but also on helping teachers learn and grow as mentors in reading. Through Learner Support, teachers gain insight into the processes that are a part of literacy learning. They also come to understand how these processes can be interrupted when children experience difficulty in some other aspect of their lives.

Kenneth, a teacher in our school, says:

"I guess my biggest question, even when I started and I'm still doing it now, is not, 'Am I doing the right thing?'; it's more, 'Am I doing all I can do?' I guess you ask yourself that all the time. Sometimes after a session that didn't go well I'll say, 'Is this really helping this child? Am I doing the right things?' I guess it's only natural to get a little frustrated when you don't see things happening as you expect to see them. So I ask myself, 'Do I keep doing the same things, or do we move on? What could I do differently to help this child?' I guess you're always going to ask yourself those kinds of questions. It's what you have to do to find the best way to work with any one child."

The Context

Regardless of grade level or area of the curriculum, facilitating learning is the role of any classroom teacher. Learner Support does not take away from what the teacher does every day with individuals or groups of various sizes. It complements and supports any classroom literacy program but it in no way takes the place of normal classroom routines or work. Nor is it meant to replace the support offered to children by reading specialists or remedial programs already in place.

Learner Support is based on an entirely different premise: That all classroom teachers who wish to do so can learn how to help children who are experiencing difficulties with their reading. The classroom teacher is the one who has the most comprehensive profile of a child's learning and who, consequently, is likely to be in the best position to help the child if learning problems arise. Much of the success of Learner Support lies in the fact that when teachers feel they are capable of helping children with problems, they are indeed able to help those children.

If you are like most classroom teachers, you have children who need extra support in learning to read. This book is intended to serve as a stepping-stone in your search to provide that support. Use the information and resource materials as best suits your situation.

We hope that the Learner Support framework will provide you with the assistance you need to help those children who challenge both your expertise and experience. With practice, a bit of organization, and a little time, both you and your children can reap the benefits of a rewarding partnership in learning.

CHAPTER 2

Understanding the Process of Reading

Reading is a highly complex problem-solving activity. For that reason, a person can only learn more about it — and become better at it — by engaging in it. Regardless of the age of the reader, the process of reading and making sense of the printed text is the same: Drawing on knowledge and experience, the reader employs a variety of strategies to construct meaning. An engaged reader practices successful strategies tirelessly to make reading a meaningful experience.

Figuring out or "decoding" words is just the tip of the reading iceberg. Reading is now seen by many educators as a transaction between reader and text, involving not only what the author has written but also what the reader brings to the text. It involves being able to bring understanding to the print, and this depends on a number of factors.

- **Purpose for Reading:** The reader's purpose greatly affects how the text is read and what the reader feels about it. The interaction of a person who is reading a text for recreation and interest differs from that of someone who is reading to meet external demands such as homework assignments or work requirements.

- **Attitude Toward Reading:** The ease or difficulty with which a person reads affects his or her interaction with the text. An individual who does not enjoy reading or who feels it is "hard work" does not have the same degree of engagement as someone who finds reading a relaxing and enjoyable occupation.

- **Ability to Summon a Repertoire of Strategies:** A reader who draws on a variety of problem-solving strategies has more opportunity to construct meaning from a text than someone who relies on one or two strategies. Readers employ many strategies — making and confirming predictions, rereading, using context or graphic cues, using graphophonic cues, and breaking words into smaller recognizable units, for example — and have many ways to figure out an unfamiliar text.

- **Background Experience and Previous Understanding:** A reader who is familiar with the subject matter of a text already has a basis for making sense of it. Background experience helps a reader to compare what is being read with what he or she already knows, and to then synthesize the text and come to a fuller understanding.

- **Knowledge of How Language Works:** A reader who is familiar with narrative patterns, language structures, jargon, and special terms finds it easier to bring meaning to a text than one who must skip over many unfamiliar terms or spend time looking them up in a reference source or asking others. Disjointed connections can disrupt the process of reading and lead to poor comprehension.

- **Ability to Use Graphic Supports:** The reader's ability to interpret and understand such supportive materials as maps, charts, diagrams, and photographs also affects understanding. Visual information often provides an additional pathway through a text.

Predicting and Confirming

Research has also made clear the important role that prediction plays in the process of reading. Experienced readers do not necessarily read every single word, phrase, or paragraph. A reader who is familiar with the language patterns of the text and who has an adequate background knowledge of the textual information is often able to predict what will come next without consciously thinking about it. As long as the predictions make sense in the context of what is being read at the time, the reader goes on, possibly not even noticing that he or she has substituted another word or phrase for what is actually in the text.

The act of prediction is an unconscious but self-regulated part of the experienced reader's process of reading. The ability to predict what word makes sense, how a phrase should end, or how to finish off a sentence without reading word for word is part of fluent reading behavior. We therefore need to teach a variety of strategies — such as brainstorming, scanning, skimming, and using pictorial evidence — to help children develop their ability to make reasonable predictions about what they are reading.

Using Language Cues and Problem-Solving Strategies

Teachers of reading need a working knowledge of language cues and the reading strategies used to make sense of print. In his discussion about the process of reading, Don Holdaway (1979) describes the following types of cues used by readers to predict meaning:

- **Semantic and Syntactic:** The reader uses context clues, both informational and grammatical, as a basis for predicting what makes sense at a particular point in the text.

- **Configurational or Featural:** The reader uses recognizable and familiar words, word patterns, or word structures to predict unknown elements.

- **Graphophonic:** The reader uses a knowledge of letter and sound relationships in order to blend sounds or small word parts into recognizable words.

At the same time that the reader is using these cuing systems to make sense of a text, he or she is using a number of problem solving strategies — what Holdaway calls "universal minor strategies." These include:

- **Rerun:** The reader goes back and rereads the sentence up to the problem word, in order to gain informational or grammatical context to help predict the word.

- **Read On:** This includes omitting or skipping the word — or blanking the word by substituting a predetermined word such as *blank* — and continuing with the reading. Later on, the reader can return to the word and try to figure it out based on subsequent text.

- **Use of Picture Clues:** The reader uses illustrations or graphic material to provide information or to help determine what word or words make sense.

- **Identify:** The reader recalls previous experiences with a word or words to make sense of the present text.

- **Compare:** The reader uses visually definable parts of a word to help figure out what it might be. In so doing, the reader makes connections between word families, notes small words in a big word, breaks a word into syllables, and uses knowledge of suffixes and prefixes.

- **Sound Out:** The reader blends letter sounds into a word or a sound combination that allows prediction of what a word might be.

- **Ask:** The reader asks for help in figuring out a text.

In using the Learner Support framework, you are sure to find that practice and knowledge will work together as you guide children through the reading process.

Janice, another teacher in our school, says:

"Sometimes I look back at what I thought reading was, and I laugh and weep at my own lack of knowledge. How could someone who loves reading as much as I do not see that it is so much more than words on a page or sounds going together in certain patterns? Reading is a complex process and readers make use of all they already know — what the text offers to them in the form of context, and their own expertise as readers. It's my job as a teacher to help children discover what they already know and find out what the author and the text have to say to them. It's great to be able to share something you enjoy doing so much with others.

Now when I help students with their reading, I encourage them to try different strategies. Really, I'm just helping them to discover what works best for them. I'm teaching them what I and other readers have been doing right along. The difference is that now I know that's how you help someone become a better reader: Practice reading and try out the strategies that all readers use."

In the process, all your training and past experience come together, influencing what you do. Sometimes theory and practice may even do battle as you adjust, reflect, and initiate procedures to respond to the needs of a particular child. It is this continual adjustment — an integration of theory and practice — that will enhance your effectiveness as a reading teacher.

CHAPTER 3

Recognizing the Children Who Need Learner Support

We often hear or read about the "at-risk" learner. That term means different things to different people, and as a result it has a wide range of connotations and definitions. Many of those connotations are negative. Nevertheless, there is no question that there are children who experience difficulty in one or more aspects of their learning. And for some, those difficulties become cumulative if learning supports are not provided at an appropriate time.

This is true for children who require help for a short time and for those who need it on a long-term basis. It is true for children who have disabilities that are organic, developmental, or emotional in origin. It is also true for children whose academic progress is not consistent with their abilities or whose progress is slower than might be expected.

At some point during their schooling, most children need extra support. In reading, this support may take the form of a single session, several sessions over the course of a few weeks, or sustained support over a longer period of time. The Learner Support framework enables teachers to provide support as a child needs it.

Generally, a teacher decides to offer extra help to a child based on observations made over time. Looking back at the reading history of a child, as well as using some forms of diagnostic testing, provides additional insight into the problems a child is having and suggests what support might be necessary.

Typical Reading Problems

Margaret Phinney's *Reading with the Troubled Reader* [see Bibliography, page 104] is one resource on which you can draw to become more familiar with the reading problems children may experience. Phinney gives a description of how such difficulties might exhibit themselves and then provides practical, teacher-tested suggestions for helping children through them. From her years of experience as a classroom teacher and a resource teacher, she believes that "troubled readers" manifest themselves in the following categories:

Overloaded Readers

These children lack the required understanding of how language works. (By language, we mean phrasing, dialogue, repetition and predictability, sentence structure, questions and answers, contractions, use of innuendo and tonal expression, and so on.) These children may also lack the experiences that provide the information and knowledge of vocabulary needed to make sense of what they are reading.

Such children are often eager to read but, since they do not have a cognitive background of information and experience to serve as a reference point, they are limited in their ability to read appropriate texts.

Underpredictive Readers

These children read word by word, trying to figure out each word by the process of decoding. They rely only on their knowledge of letter-sound relationships and see reading as the act of blending sounds and words together. These children have great difficulty fully comprehending what they read. They concentrate so much on the process of figuring out the puzzle that they are not able to put together the ideas expressed in the text.

Overpredictive Readers

These children tend to overuse strategies, such as blanking, substituting, and reading on, since their main goal is to get through the passage with as little work as possible. When they come to an unfamiliar word, they very often do not try to figure it out and may not even be willing to give it a try. They are much more comfortable moving on, and often do not notice a miscue or make any attempt to self-correct once they discover that their substitution did not make sense.

Strategy-Dependent Readers

These readers are generally able to make accurate predictions, and they try to focus on the meaning of the text; however, they have difficulty paying attention to the details in the print. They use more than one cuing system and employ different strategies, but are often unaware of, or unable to use, the subtle nuances — beginning sounds of words, differences in similar words, common word endings and beginnings, plurals, and apostrophes — that could help them focus on more accurate reading.

Global Learners

These children have difficulty remembering sight words and must use roundabout associations to figure words out. This leads to very slow reading, which interferes with comprehension. Often this kind of troubled reader comprehends complex oral stories and has a broad understanding of the world but, for reasons that are not always clear or explainable, has difficulty remembering words from one time of usage to the next.

Children with Multiple Reading Difficulties

Phinney's groupings are broad generalizations that describe reading behaviors and offer possible suggestions for intervention. Because many children have a combination of these difficulties, each child must be assessed and supported using methods appropriate for that child's individual needs, interests, and learning style. In Learner Support, one teacher works with one child using a methodology that is universal in nature but specifically adapted to build on unique strengths and meet particular needs.

Since Learner Support is mainly concerned with literacy and reading development, most of the children who are recommended for it have the same general problem: They are employing ineffective reading strategies or have reached a stage in their development where the strategies they are using — or not using — are interrupting the natural progression of their learning.

At this point we will introduce you to five children: Andrew, Tammy, Carrie, Tasha, and Charles. These children represent the kinds of readers who are candidates for Learner Support. Their reading problems differ, but in each case their classroom teacher recognized they needed extra support and accepted the challenge of trying to provide that assistance. Perhaps you will see one or more of the children you teach or have taught in these portraits. You may also find yourself identifying with the feelings and thoughts of the teachers as they seek appropriate ways to help these struggling students.

Andrew's Story

Andrew was the type of child who, according to his parents, his teachers, and even his tests, should not have had difficulty learning to read; and yet, by the end of grade 2, he was beginning to struggle. From the time he started school, Andrew had been eager to take part in theme-related activities and had participated enthusiastically during shared language sessions. He always read along, he pointed out observations about the print, and he was attentive to the stories as they were read. He had a large store of general knowledge and experiences, which he shared eagerly during discussions.

By the time he entered grade 3, however, it was apparent that Andrew was not as confident as he had once been. His teacher tried whatever she could think of to help him with his reading, including enlisting the assistance of his parents. She also gave Andrew extra sight words to practice and extra books to take home.

As the year went on, Andrew increasingly lacked interest in theme topics, and often did not complete class work or projects. He was inattentive and began getting into trouble in the classroom and on the playground. His teacher had to remind him to participate in group discussions and shared language sessions — when the teacher and students read big books and charts together. Andrew didn't want to take books out of the library or share with his parents the books he was reading at school. He seemed tired and under stress, and his health was not the best.

Through grade 4, Andrew became more and more frustrated by his inability to read the materials his classmates were reading. The cycle of failure and frustration further lowered his self-esteem. By grade 5, his parents were desperate. Neither they nor his new teacher, Martin, could understand why Andrew was having so much trouble. Andrew needed help immediately, but what kind of help? It seemed to Martin that everything had already been tried. He was at a loss to know how further help should or could be offered, but it was clear to him that no one else in the school system was going to take ownership of the problem. What did anyone have to lose if Martin tried working with Andrew in a more focused one-on-one way?

Tammy's Story

Tammy put her all into everything she did. No matter how hard something was, she stuck with it, asked for help, and continued with determination. The problem was that she always seemed to be in over her head in any discussion. She had never been to an aquarium, a large city, or a museum. She did not own many books of her own, although she cherished those her teacher had given her as gifts. She had never gone on a vacation or stayed overnight outside her immediate community. She had never ridden on a train, gone to an airport, or even been stuck in a traffic jam. Tammy could name very few places in her own community, let alone in the rest of the world.

Yet Tammy wanted to read and told her teacher that was what she wished for on a star, or when she broke the wishbone on the holiday turkey. Her teacher, Elaine, tried to help her, but she didn't seem to be making any progress — Tammy appeared to be stalled at an early emergent level. She had been kept back for an extra year in grade 1 in the hope that this would give her a chance to catch up. Although she enjoyed the extra year, it did not make any appreciable difference in Tammy's reading abilities.

Once she was in grade 2, Tammy was even more overloaded by the information she encountered. She still lacked experience and prior knowledge to bring to her reading; as a result, she continued to struggle. Elaine was concerned that, as time went on, Tammy would find herself drowning in print, unable to make sense of what her peers were handling easily. In fact, Tammy seemed to have little in common with the other children in the class. By nature a quiet child, she withdrew more and more from life in the classroom and did not participate in book talks or group project work.

She repeatedly asked Elaine to help her learn to read. Elaine felt that she was letting Tammy down, but she had no idea how to help.

Tammy was selected for Learner Support because she was ineligible for any other service. She tested too well for resource help, or for the help available to children with special needs. Her desire and determination to read also encouraged Elaine to want to try individual support which, she knew, Tammy might need all through her school career. If she could show that this child made significant gains, Elaine felt that she would be able to arrange the same kind of support from next year's teacher as well. She was as determined as Tammy to give it a try.

Carrie's Story

Carrie was a puzzle. Some days, she read the books in her book box with ease, recalling each word or phrase with little error. Other days, she halted at every other word, screwing up her face and searching for the word in some tucked-away file folder in her mind. Carrie knew that she had trouble remembering things. She would tell herself "I know that," or she would make a struggling "ah-ah-ah-ah" sound. But no matter how hard Carrie tried, the words eluded her, and she was unable to retrieve them.

Her teacher, Janice, tried giving her a word box in which she could keep new words for practice. She gave Carrie short books that used a repetition of basic vocabulary. Janice and Carrie wrote stories together using the words Carrie struggled with. Carrie continued to have trouble but not every day, however; that was what worried her teacher most. Janice wondered if there might be something wrong with the girl's vision, yet tests indicated that her sight was fine.

Carrie's mother had also noticed the same problem when she tried to help her daughter learn Bible verses for Sunday school. She noticed that Carrie would get frustrated when she could not remember and would hit the side of her head with her hand. Yet, on her good days, Carrie had very little difficulty reciting the verses.

Janice knew that right now, in grade 4, Carrie could handle her struggles with reading. Her good days were sufficiently frequent to keep her motivated and feeling a sense of progress. But Janice wondered what would happen if the good days became fewer, or if Carrie found herself with a teacher who demanded consistent performance from day to day.

This child stumped her. Janice did not know whether Carrie's difficulties would be long-term or short-term. Through Learner Support, Janice felt she might be able to determine whether this stage was a part of Carrie's natural development or something else.

Tasha's Story

Tasha was a young child who was bilingual in some respects and unilingual in others. Because she was born in the Netherlands, she had some delay in learning English and demonstrated turns of phrase and grammatical structures associated with the Dutch language. Tasha knew a number of basic sight words, but when she read, she often read word by word. When she came to an unfamiliar word, she was not able to apply any strategies to figure it out on her own.

By grade 1, Tasha already lacked self-esteem. She wanted to impress her teacher, Kenneth, with what she knew, and yet she lost confidence when she was reading. She read in an almost inaudible whisper and mumbled the words she had difficulty with. This made it very difficult for Kenneth to determine exactly what she was reading. It sounded like reading on the one hand; on the other, it seemed to be full of miscues, which went uncorrected or unnoticed.

Tasha selected only books she felt comfortable with and was able to retell these stories. But Kenneth was not convinced that Tasha understood what she read, especially new material.

Kenneth wanted to help Tasha learn to figure out unknown words from context, but didn't know how to go about it when he was unsure what, exactly, she was reading. He did not want to upset Tasha or make her feel even more unsure of herself — this would only contribute to the problem. Yet he felt that Tasha's learning was at a standstill, that she was making no appreciable progress in her reading.

Like Tammy, Tasha was stuck at an early emergent stage of reading development. Kenneth felt that individual sessions might help guide her to the next level by providing the safety net she needed to feel successful.

Charles's Story

In all respects, Charles appeared to be an average student. He participated in class discussions and activities and was confidenly outgoing. In reading, however, he blurted out responses without giving them any thought. His offhand manner gave his teacher the impression that he simply could not be bothered.

Charles seldom looked beyond the first letter of a word; he made guesses based on the pictures or what he thought he already knew. He read confidently, but seldom went back and corrected his miscues, ignoring whether his reading made sense.

In the early grades, Charles used his prediction skills to great advantage. He read by relying on his memory, and never really focused on the print in more than a casual way. By grade 3, however, his teacher Anna noticed that Charles could not read longer texts. He resisted chapter books and only wanted to read short, predictable texts. Anna was concerned because she felt that Charles was far more capable than his progress in reading indicated. She also worried about his indifferent attitude toward reading and his overreliance on emergent reading skills.

Perhaps Charles would eventually realize that he needed to use more than memory and prediction to read the books he wanted to read — or perhaps he would end up with an even greater reading problem. Anna did not want to wait to find out. She believed that, with some coaching, his reading would take off.

Selecting Candidates for Learner Support

If the children we have described seem familiar, or if the plight of their teachers strikes a chord, the Learner Support framework may provide the systematic help you need.

In deciding which children to involve, you are limited only by the amount of time you feel you can schedule into your week. For this reason, each teacher must establish personal criteria for deciding which children's needs take priority. To do so, you will want to think in particular about each child's strengths and problems, as demonstrated and recorded over time. The following six pages offer a selection of Information Gathering Tools to help you collect and organize your observations and knowledge regarding the literacy development of a student.

- Reproducible 1. **Preservice Profile.** This form offers a starting point to record your observations and knowledge of a child who may need assistance in learning to read.

- Reproducible 2. **Is This Child a Candidate for Learner Support?** This checklist serves as a basis to determine what further information you may need before determining whether a child is a suitable candidate. It can also help you to determine the criteria to use in making decisions about what children you will involve in Learner Support.

- Reproducibles 3, 4, and 5. **Teacher-Child Interview, Parts 1, 2, and 3.** These surveys are very useful in revealing children's feelings about reading, their reading strategies and preferences, their responses to books, and assessments of their own strengths and needs. This information will provide you with starting points for discussions about literacy, as well as play an integral role when you are planning extra support for a child's development.

- Reproducible 6. **Overview of Reading Behaviors.** This chart gives you a picture of a child's literacy development as well as providing an assessment tool to indicate progress over time.

1. Preservice Profile

Name _____   Date _____

What do I already know about this child as a reader? As a learner?

What questions do I have about this child as a reader? As a learner?

Student rating based on my observations and the child's history.

Ability to function on reading-related tasks:

low	average	high

Attitude toward reading:

low	average	high

Self-esteem:

low	average	high

Other comments:

2. Is This Child a Candidate for Learner Support?

Name _____ Date _____

The Child's Observable Reading Behaviors

- What are the observable indications that the child is experiencing difficulties?
- What kinds of difficulties is the child having?
- Could these difficulties be helped with individualized support?

The History of the Child as a Reader

- Is this a recent development in the child's history as a reader?
- What factors may be a cause of past or current problems?

The Child's Attitude Toward Reading

- Does the child exhibit a desire to read more effectively?
- Does the child seem frustrated when reading?
- Does the child take part in reading activities other than personal reading?

The Child's Self-Esteem

- Is the child's difficulty with reading affecting his or her behavior and attitude toward other classroom activities?
- Is the child's reading problem having a negative effect on his or her self-esteem and/or interaction with others?

The Child's Performance in Other Literacy-Related Activities

- Is the child also having difficulty in learning to write and express ideas?
- Is the child's problem with reading affecting work in other curriculum areas?
- Does the child take part in activities such as acting out stories, putting on puppet plays, retelling familiar stories, or sharing details of an experience?

The Benefits that Learner Support Might Provide to this Child

- What are the needs of this particular child at this time?
- How might Learner Support help the child overcome his or her problems?

Other Questions

- Can the child learn new strategies when working in a group?
- Does the kind of intervention the child needs require special skills I do not possess?

3. Teacher-Child Interview, Part 1

Name _____   Date _____

I'd like to know more about you. Tell me:

- about your family

- what you like to play

- what hobbies or collections you have

- who you like to spend time with

- where you like to go

- about your pets

- what you would like to learn more about

- who you would like to learn it with

4. Teacher-Child Interview, Part 2

Name _____ Date _____

I'd like to know more about how you feel about reading.

- Do you like to read?

    If "yes," what do you like to read?

    If "no," why don't you like to read?

- Do you read every day?

    If not, how often?

    When do you read?

- Does anyone read to you?

    If "yes," who?

- Who in your class is a good reader?

    How do you know this person(s) is a good reader?

- Do you think you are a good reader?

    If "yes," what makes you think so?

    If "no," what makes you think so?

- What would make you a better reader?

- When you read by yourself, what do you do when you come to a word you don't know?

- When you read by yourself, what do you do when you don't understand what you are reading?

- How do you decide what book you will read?

5. Teacher-Child Interview, Part 3

Name _____   Date _____

Attitude Survey

Place a check mark in the box that most often describes the child's reading behavior.

Key: **A** = Always   **S** = Sometimes   **N** = Never

	A	S	N
I feel good about how I read.			
I like to receive books as gifts.			
I like reading by myself.			
I learn new things when I read.			
I like to read with my mom/dad/other people.			
I feel proud when I finish reading a book.			
I think reading will help me with schoolwork.			
I think reading is fun.			
I like choosing books to read during free time.			
I like going to the library.			
I like reading to someone else.			
I like talking about books with my friends.			
I like to read books at home.			
I think it is important to be a good reader.			

6. Overview of Reading Behaviors

Name _____   Book _____

Place a check mark in the box that most often describes the child's reading behavior.

Key: **A** = Always   **S** = Sometimes   **N** = Never

	A	S	N
Use of Supportive Clues Does the child:			
● use picture clues?			
● refer back to text already read?			
Use of Reading Strategies Does the child:			
● read on?			
● predict?			
Word Identification Skills Does the child:			
● notice words within words?			
● attend to print details?			
● recall sight words?			
● use graphophonic information?			
Monitoring/Predicting/Self-Correction Does the child:			
● realize when the material he or she is reading does not make sense?			
● make connections to personal experiences or to other reading?			
● make predictions about what will happen next?			

Book-Handling Knowledge

The background experiences that children have had with books are indicators of future success in the school environment, as well as keys to planning instruction for students. The book-handling knowledge task, adapted by Goodman and Altwerger from work by M. Clay (1973) and D. Doake (1977), allows the teacher valuable insights into the experiential base from which the child operates. This task, combined with print-awareness tasks, is helpful for evaluating the child's emerging knowledge of literacy and is useful with children who cannot successfully make sense of continuous text. It focuses on directionality, use or understanding of terminology such as page, letter, and word, and concepts concerning the source of language. It shows the familiarity children have with books, their knowledge about the function of print in books, and their use of language related to print in books.

Guidelines for Using the Book-Handling Task

1. Take a picture storybook that is suitable for a beginning reader.

2. Make sure that the book has a title page with the book title and author's name.

3. Make sure that the pages have clear, bold print and that there are many illustrations. If possible, choose a book with a page of print on one side and an illustration on the other.

4. If you are right-handed, sit with the child on your left, and vice versa if you are left-handed.

5. Try not to give the child too much information or direction. If a child cannot read or refuses to read, then read the book to him or her.

7. Book-Handling Knowledge Task, Part 1

Name _____   Book _____

Item	Administration	Instruction	Response	Child's Response
1	Show book; title covered by hand. Flip over pages.	"What's this called?" If child answers with the name of the book, record and ask, "What's [say name of book given by child]?	"Book." "Storybook." "Story." "Name of book."	
2	Displaying book.	"What do you do with it?"	"Read it." "Look at it." "Tell it." "Open it."	
3	Displaying book.	"What's inside it?"	"Story." "Pictures." "Words." "Pages." "Letters." "Things."	
4	Present book wrong way up and back toward child.	"Show me the front of this book." "Take the book and open it so that we can read it together."	Any indication of front or first page.	
5	Turn to page 3.	Hold on to a page and say, "Show me a page in this book." "Is this a page?"	Points to page; "Yes."	
6	Give the book to child.	"Read this to me."	[Record all responses.]	
7	If child doesn't read the book or does inappropriate book reading, continue: Give the book to the child; read the first page.	"I'm going to read you this story. You show me where to start reading." "Where do I begin?"	Indicates print on first page.	
8	Turn to next page.	"Show me the top of this page." "Show me the bottom of this page."	Indicates top edge or toward top; indicates bottom of page or toward bottom.	

8. Book-Handling Knowledge Task, Part 2

Name _____ Date _____

Item	Administration	Instruction	Response	Child's Response
9	Show the page to the child.	"Show me with your finger exactly where I begin reading."	Points to the to first word on the page.	
10	Show the page to the child.	"Show me with your finger which way I go as I read this page."	Left to right, on the page.	
11	Continue to show the page to the child.	"Where then?" [This may already have been done or stated in #9; if so, credit, but do not repeat.]	Top line to bottom line.	
12	Read the page.	"You point to the story while I read it." [Read slowly.]	Exact matching of spoken word with written word; close matching.	
13	If there is print on both pages, display the pages.	"Where do I go now?"	Points to the first line of print on the next page.	
14	Read the next two pages. If possible, turn to a page with print and a picture on it. Turn the book upside down without the child seeing you.	"Can you or I read this now? Why or why not?"	Says the book is upside down.	
15	Show child how to use masking card to close the "curtains" over the "window." [Use two pieces of black cardboard.]	"Let's put some of the story in this window. I want you to close the curtains like this until I can see *just one letter*. "Now just *two* letters."	One letter correct; two letters correct.	
16	Open "curtains."	"Now close it until we can see *just one word*." "Now just *two* words."	One word correct; two words correct.	

9. Book-Handling Knowledge Task, Part 3

Name _____ Date _____

Item	Administration	Instruction	Response	Child's Response
17	Open "curtains."	"Show me the first letter in a word — any word."	First correct; last correct.	
18	Remove card.	"Show me a capital letter — any capital letter."	Points clearly to a capital letter; points to any capital letter.	
19	Read to end of story; close book and pass it to the child.	"Show me the name of the book [or the name of the story.]"	Cover, flyleaf, or title page.	
20	Get at comprehension.	"Tell me something about the story."		
21	Leave the book with the child.	"Show me the beginning of the story." "Show me the end of the story."	Opens book to first page and points to the first line; turns to last page and points to the last line.	
22	Title page pointing.	"It says here [read title of the book] by [read author's name]. What does it mean?"	"[S]he wrote it." "[S]he made up it up." "[S]he made the book."	

Miscue Analysis

Miscue analysis assists teachers in observing and recording a child's reading behaviors. Originally described in Goodman and Burke (1972), a miscue analysis on the reading of a passage by a child allows you to assess the learner's ability to:

• make graphophonic connections
• use strategies and cuing systems to construct meaning from print
• comprehend and analyze information presented in the text
• show understanding of what has been read

Using a shortened version of the original Miscue Analysis format can help you gain an initial sense of the strategies a child is using and also provide information necessary to plan for future Learner Support sessions. If you tape your session with a child, you can refer back to it later for a more in-depth assessment of the child's reading strategies.

Begin by having the child read a slightly challenging text, and note what he or she does while reading. Whenever a child's reading differs from the printed text, mark up a copy of the text using shorthand symbols such as:

Substitution: Write substituted word above line of print.

Self-Correction: Write and circle (SC) for a self-correction, (UC) for an unsuccessful correction.

Omission: Circle word(s) or punctuation omitted.

Insertion: Use caret (∧) and write inserted word.

Reversal: Use an arrow or transposition mark (the book) to show how words were read.

Repetition: Underline repeated text.

After the reading, discuss the text, encouraging the child to make inferences and personal connections to the text. You may also wish to have the child retell the story as a comprehension check.

As you review the taped reading, consider whether the reader's miscues affected meaning and how and why the reading self-corrected. By looking at the kinds of miscues, you will be able to tell which reading strategies and cuing systems the child is using and not using. The number of miscues will allow you to make inferences and decisions as to the appropriate kinds and levels of reading materials you should use with the child.

10. Miscue Analysis

Choose a reading selection whose level of difficulty challenges the student's independent reading level. You may need to have the student attempt several pieces until reading fluency decreases. Then have the student read from the book while you record miscues and strategies used. An oral retelling is a useful comprehension check.

Title of Selection: _____

Miscue Summary

with no meaning loss (type, number, and comments):

with meaning loss (type, number, and comments):

Reading Strategies/Cuing Systems

Comments on Student Retelling:

Running Record

Perhaps one of the most effective evaluation tools for providing insight into a child's use of reading strategies is the running record. Doing a running record requires no prior preparation of materials, special recording sheets, or previous training on your part. You simply use an easy shorthand to record the strategies a child employs while dealing with a text. You can use a running record with any book the child is reading, recording it directly into your teacher's diary. If need be, you can analyze it in greater depth following the session. If you take a running record once a week, the information you gather will provide a profile of the child's reading progress that you can use for both planning sessions and discussions with parents.

The procedure is easy to use; you can teach yourself to do it. Use the shorthand symbols on the chart or develop your own.

Running Record Shorthand

Accurately reads	✔
Substitution	$\dfrac{\text{child's word}}{\text{actual word in text}}$
Repetition	**R**
Return and Repetition	✔✔✔ R
Self-Correction	**SC**
Omission	$\dfrac{\bullet}{\text{actual word in text}}$
Insertion	$\dfrac{\text{child's inserted word}}{\bullet}$
Pause (or delay in response)	/ (# of seconds)
Child asks for help	word in text | ?
Child waits for help	word in text | W (child looks at teacher expecting help)
Teacher tells child word	word in text | T

As you examine the child's miscues after the reading, ask yourself if the error or self-correction was one of:

- **meaning** (context, background knowledge, literal and figurative associations)
- **structure** (word order, sentence structure)
- **visual** (letter/sound relationships, letter clusters)

Use shorthand **M**, **S**, or **V** for each miscue or self-correction.

Other Useful Information

Any information that provides insight into literacy-related aspects of a child's development can be helpful when you are deciding whether a child could benefit from Learner Support. As the classroom teacher, you will already have gathered, in your informal observations of the child, much of the information you need to help you make that decision. Other materials that can provide you with insight include:

- a list of books the child has read
- copies of reading logs or book reports
- samples of writing
- your own notes on how the child responds to literacy activities
- information about how the family supports the child's learning
- information regarding the child's interests

Any information you gather will be helpful when making your decision as to whether or not a child is a suitable candidate. Once you have decided to work with a child, the same information will also provide you with insights into how you can best support the child's next step toward becoming an independent reader.

Sample Running Records

Accurate

On Monday I went for a walk. ✔✔✔✔✔✔

(One check for each word accurately read.)

Substitutions

On Monday I went for a walk. ✔✔✔ $\frac{walked}{went}$ ✔✔ $\frac{while}{walked}$

Repititions

On Monday I went for a walk. ✔✔✔ R ✔✔✔

(Child rereads the word *went*, then reads on.)

↰ ✔✔✔✔ R ✔✔✔

(Child reads the word *went*, then returns to the beginning of the sentence and reads again.)

↰ ✔✔✔✔ R₂ ✔✔✔

(As above, but child repeats reading 2 times (R3 – 3 times, etc.)

Self-Corrections

On Monday I went for a walk. ✔✔✔ $\frac{walked}{went}$ | SC ✔✔✔

(Record word child uses with **SC** notation.)

Omissions

On Monday I went for a walk. ✔✔✔ $\frac{\bullet}{went}$ ✔✔✔

(Use ● over the text to indicate word left out.)

Insertions

On Monday I went for a walk. ✔✔✔✔✔✔ $\frac{long}{\bullet}$ ✔

(Record word child adds over ____ .)

Try Again

Use when you know the child can read more of the text than appears or when the child does not seem to be giving a best effort.)

On Monday I went for a walk. ✔$\frac{morning}{Monday}$ ✔ $\frac{wake}{went}$ $\frac{father}{for}$ ✔✔ (TA) ✔✔✔✔✔✔✔

(Record first try, then **Try Again** followed by second try.)

Child Asks For Help / Teacher Gives Word

On Monday I went for a walk. ✔ $\frac{}{Monday}$ | $\frac{?}{T}$ ✔✔✔✔✔

(Child asks for help; teacher tells child the word.)

CHAPTER 4

Planning For Sessions

ust as you make decisions all the time regarding your classroom organization and its curriculum, you will also make Learner Support decisions on a continual basis. Most of the planning is in organizing the program: arranging time, space, and materials; preparing appropriate recording tools; selecting the children; and gathering books to meet their specific needs.

> **"** When you are working with kids in these sessions, you have to be able to make decisions based on what you see happening, and at first that felt overwhelming. Then I realized I didn't have to make those decisions right on the spot. If I wasn't sure what to do, I could do some research, like go back to Margaret Phinney's book, or I could talk to other teachers about it and find out if they had ever met up with a similar situation. You have to make decisions, but after a little practice and with a little support, you begin to feel more confident about your decisions and what you are doing. **"**
>
> **—Elaine, grade 2 teacher**

> **"** When we first started implementing Learner Support, I had no idea how I was going to find time or energy to do even more planning and scheduling, especially for one individual student at a time. It was quite a relief and even a surprise to find out that it didn't require that much time at all. Once the program got rolling, the planning was actually quite easy. Each session just sort of grows out of the last one. **"**
>
> **—Anna, grade 2 teacher**

Organizing Time, Space, and Materials

Once you establish a basic structure for the sessions and a firm commitment to time, your planning becomes efficient and suited to each child's needs. Deciding what to do in successive sessions principally involves looking at what was done in previous ones and continuing from there. Also, as you work with the children individually, you will get a clearer picture of their overall strengths and needs, and consequently find it easier to help them participate fully in classroom activities.

When you are starting out, you need to be realistic about the amount of time you can set aside for sessions each day. This will help you to decide the number of students to include, so that you can establish a workable schedule. You will also need to decide where to conduct your sessions. Although it is not necessary to designate a special area of the classroom, it is often more efficient to have one place where materials are stored and work is done.

The materials you gather ahead of time will depend on your initial plans and the needs of the children — whatever you or the children might need that will help you to make the best use of your time together. Helpful items to include are a few professional references, your teaching and recording tools, a folder of some kind for each child, and a variety of writing and other resource materials for the children to use.

Preparing Planning and Record-Keeping Tools

Devising appropriate planning and record-keeping tools and procedures is the next important step in preparing for strategy sessions. For example, you will need a diary in which to make notes about each session. You, and perhaps the student, will want to keep a log of the books the child has read, so that both of you will be able to see the expanding numbers and increasing complexity of those books. Also, a pass-along book helps to keep the child's family informed about what is happening in Learner Support and encourages their comments and participation.

The Teacher's Diary

The teacher's diary is an important tool for planning strategy sessions. In the diary, you can record your observations of what happens in each session.

You may want to start out with a more formal structure for recording information about sessions. The reproducibles on pages 44 and 45 can serve as starting points in determining what kind of record works best for you. These are particularly useful if you anticipate that a child might require Learner Support for an extended period of time.

If you decide to use a diarylike format, you can record the date, details of what was read, notations on the child's use of strategies, and suggestions for follow-up in future sessions. Loose-leaf pages in a three-ring binder, a notebook, or a hardbound journal book all work equally well. Once you implement Learner Support, you will find the method that is the best and most efficient for you.

The following examples show some kinds of notes that Learner Support teachers find useful.

March 4
Mike and the Magic Cookies —
on 2 syllable words   p. 9 for/from
still needs reminding to monitor meaning
and not try to second-guess what the
author wants to say.

March 9 page 16
pp. 16–20 — once directed to look at
word in a word, he got the word.
next time: graded passages

March 11
2 pages read well; self-correcting; was
very noisy in the room, which broke
concentration a bit; however, he managed
to stay focused on the story.

March Break

March 23
anxious to read on in book. Rate
improved. I wouldn't let him look ahead.
It's killing him!

March 25 to p. 43
self-corrected often. "But what happens to
the wizard?" When reading *Gorillas*, was
ready to quit; however, finally noticed it
down the page — reread it and got the
word. "Oh, that's gorilla."

March 30
good self-correction — long vowels.
"Look, I got my puzzle all done."
Took *Mike and the Magic Cookies* home
to read.

Jan. 25 **Woosh!**	doing quite well with this — needs some help with beginning sounds — reminded what sound is — looked back to see word she was unsure of that she knew earlier (i.e., kicked HTS)
Jan. 27 sight words	– <u>ay</u> family – some difficulty with these – <u>get</u>, <u>his</u>, <u>got</u> – once learned <u>get</u> & <u>got</u>, able to distinguish between the two – <u>ick</u> family – unsure of this group – <u>at</u> family – unsure of this group – <u>andy</u> family – had no difficulty with this group
Feb. 1 A Lump in my Bed	looked through together talking about pictures, buildings, vocabulary — such as *touched, pulled, poked* then we read through the book; she chimed in along with me. After the reading, she worked through the story on her own.

11. Learner Support Planner

Name _____ Teacher _____

Date	Working Toward	Planned Action	Materials	Comments

11. Conference Log

Name _____ Interests _____

Date	Book	Comments	Action

Book(s) read: since last conference

Comment: noteworthy details of attitude, application, comprehension, oral reading, or activities

Action: guidance given, practice work or activities set, plans

The Reading Log

Reading logs provide a visible record to readers of the growing number of books over which they have control. How the logs are used and how much the children record in them depends on the teacher and the child, but neither the making of the log nor the recording process should take too much time. You may also wish to have the children record the author's name and perhaps a brief comment, but the log should never take the form of a book report; rather, it should be a quick and efficient means to keep an ongoing and ever-growing record of the child's reading accomplishments. Each book that a child reads is one more rung on the ladder of reading success and of the child's developing self-esteem as a reader. A reading log, no matter what the format, lets the child see progress.

Often the most effective reading logs are those the children design and make themselves. These logs can take many forms, and certain types seem to be best suited for different age groups. It's important to remember that, regardless of the age or ability of the child, keeping the log should not be a chore or detract from the actual reading.

Younger Children (ages five to eight)

For these children, a trifolded record sheet is efficient and effective. To make this, fold a piece of letter-sized paper into three sections. On each of the inside panels, put a list of numbers down the left-hand side, with a line where you or the child can write the name of the book. You can make several of these record sheets quickly by photocopying one side of your original with its three panels of numbers. For some children, drawing the cover gives them a sense of ownership and encourages them to record the books they read. Once the reading log is filled, it is an easy job to photocopy it for the child's portfolio before sending the original home.

Older Children (ages nine to twelve)

Composition books are good for children in this age group. One that is blank at the top of each page, with several lines at the bottom, works very well. Children who are reading longer books with more developed story lines can record the title at the bottom of the page, along with the date it was read. They can use the top part as a response journal, perhaps answering a question, or drawing a picture of a favorite part of the story, an interesting character, or another element.

You may wish to consider keeping a "Books We've Read" list taped to the wall, where you and the students record the title, author, and a brief comment about each book. When students see teachers' active reading lives, they are motivated to read.

13. Reading Log

Name _____ Date _____

1. _____
2. _____
3. _____
4. _____
5. _____
6. _____
7. _____
8. _____
9. _____
10. _____

11. _____
12. _____
13. _____
14. _____
15. _____
16. _____
17. _____
18. _____
19. _____
20. _____

The Pass-Along Book

As you plan for Learner Support, you will want to secure and maintain parental support and involvement. We have found a pass-along book, a notebook that travels back and forth between teacher and family, is a very effective method.

The pass-along book provides parents with an up-to-date account of what their child is doing. The notes teachers make, often in a blank hardcover book with lined pages, are usually informal in style, short to read, and positive in nature. Ongoing communication of this sort works to overcome some parental fears about the child's development. It also can allay the feeling that the family is cut off from what is going on in the school.

The following examples give you an idea of the kinds of notes that travel back and forth in the pass-along books. As you come to know the children and parents, you can judge better the kinds of support you can ask and expect from parents, how they will interpret and act on your comments, and how best to communicate with each family.

October 8

Just a note to say how relieved I am that Louise is going to get extra help in reading. She is not reading where she should be so this is great! I want her to get all the help she can get. I will do my part here at home. I noticed that you are working on different sounds. That is great.

Greg S.

October 17

Dear Greg,

Today, Louise filled me in on the chapter you read together last night. She remembered quite a lot of detail. She really seems to enjoy the book — she even wrote about it in her journal. We also worked on the long "a" sound. At first she seemed a bit confused in distinguishing sounds, but we'll continue to work on this!

She also has a few new word cards and the remainder of Chapter 6 to work on for Monday. Thanks,

Kenneth

November 16

Hello again!

It was great to meet you and to come to a consensus as to how we are going to help Louise so as not to confuse her.

When Louise and I were reviewing our list today, she said you were doing it at home. Just a reminder that at the meeting we agreed to use the list only as a reference, not as a reading lesson. It's important that when you read together at home, it's an enjoyable experience!

Thanks,

Kenneth.

December 11

Hi!

Just a note to let you know how impressed I was with Louise's reading today. She was able to figure out most of the words independently from context. When she didn't understand a paragraph, she stopped and reread silently until she was able to figure things out. Great things are beginning to happen!

Kenneth.

Four Steps

You are now ready to work with individual children. The only thing left is...
to begin.

1. Select the Children

At this point you will need to decide which child/children you are going to
work with. Your classroom experience with the children, as well as the
assessment work already done, will help you decide not only which children
might benefit from Learner Support but also which needs are most urgent.
After you establish a workable schedule, set priorities and select those
children you plan to work with first.

2. Gather the Books

To select appropriate books, you need some knowledge about children's
books in general, about the suitability of specific books for those with whom
you are working, and about the way particular elements in a book can help to
highlight the reading strategy on which you want to focus.

For example, when Elaine began to make her plans for working with
Tammy, she knew that Tammy would need help in obtaining some of the
background she lacked. Elaine established a plan for finding out more about
Tammy's hobbies and what interested her. To profile the child's reading
interests, she decided to use a reading inventory and information from her
teacher-child interviews (see pages 26-28). She then found reading material
for which Tammy would have background knowledge, allowing the child to
focus on other reading strategies.

During the first session, Elaine explained to Tammy that each time they met
they would work together on two kinds of books. First Tammy would read
one she already knew, and then she would try a new one from her book box
so that she could learn new information, find meanings for new words, and
practice new strategies.

Charles's needs were different from Tammy's. When his teacher, Anna, listened to him read, she observed that Charles seldom looked at the print. He would comb the pictures looking for possible clues to the text, or just take a guess, not even looking at the book. Anna knew she would have to get Charles to focus on the print and realize that it was an important part of the book. Anna would also have to contend with Charles's reluctance to choose longer texts. She wanted him to read longer texts, but because he wanted to read them, not because she made him.

Anna looked over the shorter predictable books in the school and found a few that fit her needs: They had only a little text, but what there was did not allow for help from the pictures. Anna also selected a few books that resembled chapter books but had large type and extremely simple vocabulary. Then she included a couple of books that were longer still, with few pictures, but with a humorous slant that would appeal to Charles's sense of humor. Anna chose twelve books in all and decided to let Charles select the ones he wanted to work on, in whatever order suited him. Her only stipulation was that he must read the whole pile before adding new titles. Anna knew that Charles would probably start with the shorter books, but sooner or later he would have to give the chapter books a try!

When you are making choices about what books to use with each child, there are a few things to keep in mind. Early readers need books in a suitable format, attractive, well organized, and with a high-quality text. Look for fiction and nonfiction in a variety of genres, books with rhyme and without, and books with colorful art or different typefaces. If you select different kinds of texts, the child will be able to practice choosing appropriate strategies in a variety of reading situations. As Marie Clay (1991) writes, a steady diet of one type of text may lead children to make false assumptions about reading.

The books that you select should be of manageable length and have subject matter that appeals to the child. Bookstores and libraries and even the resource shelves in your school are filled with books that should meet the needs and interests of all your children.

3. Judge the Child's Level of Sophistication

The simplest books are concept books. At the earliest level, these are books that supply labels for concrete objects. Usually the illustrations are uncluttered, with the text and illustrations placed consistently on the pages. These books help children learn that print carries a message, a first step toward literacy. They also encourage children to begin to correlate sounds and letters. At a more advanced level, concept books present information about nonfiction topics in a straightforward manner and format.

Slightly more complex texts are about the world of childhood and situations that are familiar to young children. They may contain refrains, rhymes, and repetitive language patterns, or they may have short sentences that reflect the syntax of the oral language structures of young children. Using these books, children begin to learn about the directionality of print. They start to use pictures as clues to meaning. They draw on their knowledge of events in their lives, on their understanding of what language sounds like, and on the predictability of rhyme and rhythm to decide what the text says.

As texts become even more complex, they contain more of the following features:

- twists on the repetitive patterns
- sentences and texts that are not patterned
- text that cannot be predicted from the illustrations
- illustrations that extend the written text
- longer sentences that reflect written rather than oral language
- more written text per page, from two or more sentences to a full page of text
- more characters, and more fully developed characters
- events that extend over two or more pages
- a plot containing a sequence of events
- more description
- increasingly sophisticated vocabulary
- idiomatic language
- a broader number of genres, such as exposition and fantasy

Books that are easy to read are also available for older children who are reading at a lower level but who must feel that they have real books to read. Look for books the size of novels but with print a little larger than usual for older children. A few pictures help, as does an attractive cover.

4. Match Books to a Child's Needs

As you are selecting books, keep in mind that reading involves a transaction between reader and text. Children with limited background knowledge and experience are likely to find some books unmanageable, even though those books may have a low readability level and would normally be considered simple. For that reason, always take your cue from the child. Choose books with which he or she has had some prior experience, which will meet an established interest, or which include a large number of sight words already in the child's repertoire.

If you are uncertain, try the child on a succession of progressively more difficult books until you find a starting point. For Learner Support sessions, begin working with a book that is a bit challenging. If the child can already read a book fluently, you will not be able to coach him or her in the use of strategies. At the same time, if every sentence is a major struggle, and the child needs coaching on every page, then using context and reading for meaning will be impossible, and the child will feel frustrated.

You need to strike the right balance for each child, providing both a safety net of familiarity and a challenge. As the child gains control over the books in his or her collection, change some of the easier ones. There should always be at least one book the child can read fluently, two on which he or she is currently working, and one that has not yet been read during a Learner Support session.

You may want to extend the original collection. For example, it may be appropriate to build an additional set of books that the child feels competent reading. Or it may be necessary to create a collection of books whose patterns are repetitive, or whose pictures support changes within the pattern, to convince a doubting child that he or she can read. Nothing is written in stone. If you discover that a book you have selected is not appropriate for the child, eliminate it. You can easily make another selection that is more or less challenging, or that is more precisely geared to the child's interests. This is what fluent readers do.

Listening to your students and learning as much as you can about their needs and interests is the best possible way to discern which books will present the right amount of challenge and positive reinforcement for them.

You may gain further insight into how to select appropriate books by reflecting on how the teachers of Tasha, Tammy, Charles, Carrie, and Andrew went about choosing their books.

Tasha's Story

One of the main considerations in Kenneth's mind as he chose books for Tasha was that he needed some that drew attention to print details. He wanted to use books with repetitive patterns and picture clues to help Tasha make sense of what she was reading, but the story also had to encourage her to attend to the print. It needed to be at a level that allowed her to feel successful, since building her confidence was a crucial issue.

One of the first books Kenneth found was *Bath Time*, by Sandra Iversen. He knew that because Tasha had a dog, she would enjoy the book, and that she would be able to read most of it using the pictures as clues. He also felt that the use of two forms of the same verb — get and gets — would be a good starting point for drawing Tasha's attention to a detail of print.

Sssh!, by Jan McPherson, also encourages a focus on the print. Tasha was immediately drawn to the pictures and enjoyed talking about what was happening. As she read, she said "Sssh!" expressively each time, repeating it and stretching it out in response to the changing text on the last page. Kenneth felt the pattern gave her security, but the nuances of the changing text encouraged her to pay close attention to the print.

A question-and-answer book by Helen Depree, called *What Do I See in the Garden?*, included rhyming pairs of words on the same page — *thinking* and *slinking*, and *creeping* and *leaping*. This encouraged Tasha to look carefully at the text to help figure out the words.

The way *The Storm*, by Jackie Goodyear, plays around with text — with the words *splish, splash, boom,* for example — made it another suitable choice. As Tasha read, Kenneth encouraged her to say the words expressively. After reading this book, Kenneth and Tasha tried playing around with some other words on large chart paper.

As Tasha progressed, Kenneth chose books like *The Rain and The Sun*, by Alan Trussell-Cullen. The text of this book is less patterned, but Kenneth felt that the story line would capture Tasha's imagination, as it did. As she read through the book, the two of them talked about what was happening in the pictures. She was beginning to gain confidence in herself as a reader, and to make connections between the stories she was reading and her own experiences.

A rebus story by Shirley Neitzel, *The Jacket I Wear in the Snow*, was a perfect book for Tasha to move into at a later date. She loved the cumulative format and worked very hard not just to guess at what the words said, but to read them carefully. This book inspired her to begin writing her own rebus stories and to share them with both Kenneth and her classmates.

Tammy's Story

As Elaine chose books for Tammy, she had to keep in mind the child's limited background experiences. She needed books that were familiar to Tammy and would allow her to gain confidence through the process of rereading. She also looked for books that would introduce new concepts and/or provide new information to expand Tammy's knowledge.

Elaine knew Tammy loved to cook so she found a "cooking" book for her: *Fruit Salad*, by Helen Depree. Its repeating pattern and the clues in the illustrations provided Tammy with the support she needed as she read the book for the first time. It was a great confidence booster.

Since Tammy's class had just learned how to use a CD-ROM program on the San Diego Zoo, Elaine felt that *The Zoo*, by Christine Young, was a good choice. Because the text is supported by photographs, once again Tammy's first read was highly successful. She was getting a taste of what it was like to read a book independently for enjoyment.

In her search for concept books that provide information, Elaine found the question-and-answer book *What Season Is This?*, by Robin Workman. As Tammy read the book for the first time, she and Elaine talked about how and why the colors of leaves change in the fall. When they got to the last page, Tammy was unsure of the word *autumn*, but because of their discussions, she was encouraged to draw on her own experiences. When Elaine prompted her by saying, "It's another word for *fall*," Tammy was able to get it.

Because Tammy loved riddles and jokes, *What Am I?*, by Brian and Jillian Cutting, was another suitable book. Its repetitive pattern, along with the clues that help readers find the answer to each riddle, helped Tammy with difficult words.

As Tammy progressed, Elaine continued to look for books that would allow her to draw on her own experiences while introducing new words and concepts. *I'm Looking for My Hat*, by Arthur Speer, was based on a familiar situation, so it was another sound choice. Tammy was able to figure out words such as *cupboard* and *laundry* and *pantry* by looking at the pictures and responding to the prompts Elaine gave.

The humorous situations in *I'm too small. YOU'RE TOO BIG.*, by Judi Barrett, made it another good choice for Tammy. After reading the first few pages, she was able to use her knowledge of the structure of the book to figure out what was happening in the text. The book was also a good model for a similar story about Tammy and her mom that Tammy wrote, with Elaine, during class writing time. She then practiced this book too, and took it home to share with her mother.

Charles's Story

Anna knew that it was important to choose books for Charles that were close to his independent reading level and that he would want to read books that were humorous, or that he perceived would be easy to read. In the beginning he balked at reading many of the books his teacher had chosen. She finally suggested that they create his collection together: He could choose one and then she would choose one until they had assembled ten titles. Naturally, the ones Charles chose had little print and lots of pictures, or were ones he had read before. Those Anna chose were slightly longer, books she thought might tickle his funny bone or pique his interest.

One book Charles chose was *Where's Sylvester's Bed?*, by JoAnn Balasek. It is a story about a large yellow tabby cat who is comfortable sleeping anywhere. Anna knew that since Charles had such a cat, this book would be a hit. Though it had large print and few sentences on the page, Charles was unaware that it would nontheless challenge him to make sense of the text.

Anna chose *Don't Panic*, by Helen Depree, even though it had lots of pictures and only a moderate amount of text, as a confidence booster. She had also heard a conversation between Charles and a classmate about the panic his dad had been in that morning when he thought he had lost his car keys. Anna knew this book would grab Charles's attention — as it did.

Jennifer Pockets, by Jan McPherson, is just plain silly. The pictures are fun and the words are playful. Anna's goal was to make reading pleasurable, and books such as this filled the bill. Also, its text helped Charles continue to develop meaning-making strategies.

Anna chose *A Clean House for Mole and Mouse*, by Harriet Ziefert, when she thought Charles was ready to move into longer texts. It has the look and feel of a longer book but still has relatively little text. The cartoonlike pictures appealed to him.

As time went on, Anna chose more books that had the look of being longer and more like chapter books. *Come Out and Play, Little Mouse*, by Robert Kraus, is a kind of diary in which the cat asks the mouse each day to come out and play and the mouse replies with some excuse. Another choice, the chapter book *Camp Big Paw*, by Doug Cushman, focuses on Cyril the Cat's first summer at camp. Its larger print and comiclike pictures mask the fact that it has a fairly long text.

Carrie's Story

Janice knew that, in the beginning, the more predictable the structure or text of the books she chose the better, since that would allow Carrie to use her ability to remember whole texts, even though she might have difficulty with the parts. Janice found a set of Eureka Treasure Chest books, originally from Australia, and discovered some titles in it that were predictable and well supported by pictures and graphics.

There's No Place Like Home, by Marc Brown, has colorful illustrations and a rhyming pattern that make it fun to read. The way the story is written, as a series of rhyming couplets, helped Carrie to develop a strategy for remembering each pair of words.

Arthur's Nose, also by Marc Brown, is about an anteater who does not like his long nose. Janice selected this book because it was written by an author familiar to Carrie and because she felt that its contents and format, with a few simple prompts, would help support Carrie's reading of the text.

When the class started its mystery theme, Janice selected *Nate the Great and the Phony Clue*, by Marjorie Weinman Sharmat. Its predictable structure helped Carrie with individual words. She and Janice worked together to make a map of the characters, and Carrie drew pictures for it. This helped her remember each name when she came to it in the text. When she forgot, a quick look at her map provided the association she needed to retrieve the word. She went on to read other books in this series as well.

Janice chose *Owl at Home* and several other books by Arnold Lobel — *Frog and Toad* and *Mouse Soup*, for example — because they contain a series of short stories within a larger context. These gave Carrie the benefit of reading manageable bits of text while developing the feeling of reading a longer book, like her peers.

Eliza the Hypnotizer, by Michele Granger, was a book Janice found as she continued to look for novels with shorter stories within them — a technique that provided Carrie with connections she could make between stories and characters.

Carrie discovered *Pet-Sitters Plus Five*, by Tricia Springstubb, at the school's book fair. She was determined to read it and asked Janice if they could use it as a Learner Support book. Janice agreed and soon found that, because Carrie had such a desire to read it, she was developing her own strategies to help her remember words: For example, she used her friend Katy's name to retrieve the word kitten, since Katy had a kitten.

Andrew's Story

When choosing a collection for Andrew, Martin looked for books that were predictable in nature yet mature enough to maintain a grade 5 child's self-esteem; Andrew would not feel comfortable with anything that was obviously for "little kids." Martin knew that in the beginning he would not be able to choose books that were close to Andrew's independent reading level. In fact, he was prepared to use techniques like assisted reading to support Andrew's early attempts.

An early choice was *Nate the Great*, by Marjorie Weinman Sharmat, a well-known book that is read by children at the grade 2 level. Although it is a chapter book, it has some predictable characteristics. Martin saw it contained many of the sight words that Andrew knew, and that it would therefore encourage the use of strategies other than sounding out.

Martin chose a short novel called *Dragons Don't Read Books*, by Brenda Bellingham. He liked the use of short bits of description and the well-written dialogue, and felt the situation — a developing friendship between a boy and a girl — was something Andrew was very close to at that point.

Secret Land of the Past is an action-packed novel, by Mirian Schlein, in which two children enter a cave hole and find themselves among animals of the past. It served as a perfect link to other time-travel stories that Andrew had enjoyed earlier. The level was a bit more challenging, but because it had some similarities to that earlier reading, he was able to tackle it successfully. By this point Martin had reduced the number of sessions with Andrew to two per week.

Martin had noticed that Andrew reverted to his old sounding-out habit whenever he read nonfiction material and, before moving him off Learner Support and onto a monitoring schedule, Martin wanted to be sure that Andrew could also tackle nonfiction text successfully. He decided to use *Gorillas*, by Patricia Demuth, while the class was working on a unit on endangered species. This book uses a combination of illustrations and photographs to support the information. Because it was so closely connected to what was happening in the classroom, Andrew did not seem to feel it was too babyish for him. He read it with great enthusiasm and sense of purpose.

A little later, when the class was working on a sea theme, Andrew chose manatees as his project topic, Martin decided that he might enjoy tackling *Dancing with Manatees*, by Faith McNulty. The text is longer but still manageable.

* * *

Even though the selections we have described were all successful choices for the children they were intended to help, some books may not be. Keep in mind that you have to make adjustments along the way, no matter how carefully you select ahead of time. Sometimes what seems like the perfect book to meet a particular child's needs or interests proves to be an absolute failure. If that happens, simply set the book aside and find a new one.

CHAPTER 5

Conducting a Session

No two children are alike, and how to best help each child depends upon you and the child. Although, like many teachers, you may initially feel apprehensive about knowing what to do and whether you will be able to help children effectively, you'll soon see that your intervention can make a difference.

> I wasn't exactly sure of what I was supposed to do at first. I must admit I was a little scared of trying to focus on reading strategies in a one-on-one situation. I was hesitant during the first couple of sessions. I was scared I would say the wrong thing or speak too quickly or not say something soon enough. But after a couple of meetings, I felt better about what I was doing. When I could see that most of it really was common sense and natural instinct, I felt much better. Mind you, I know I still need to learn more about reading strategies and the best way to help the children learn how to use them, but it's coming and we're making progress, so I feel quite good about how we work together now.
>
> **—Elaine, grade 2 teacher**

Schedule Learner Support sessions into the school day as part of regular classroom activities, generally two or three times a week. Divide these 15-minute a session into three parts, focusing the child on reading, revisiting familiar books, and beginning work on new strategies and text.

The First Session

In the first session, begin to develop a way of working with the child. You may want to talk with the child about:

- what Learner Support is
- how often sessions will be scheduled
- how long each session will be
- what you have noticed that he or she needs help with
- how you are going to work together

Outline how each session will work and explain that you will be making notes so that you can keep track of how to help in future sessions. Remember also to leave some time to answer whatever questions the child might have.

Often, a child who is having difficulty may also have low self–esteem. During the first session, you can reassure your student that you are interested in helping him or her become a better reader and that this is time you have scheduled just for him or her. Once it becomes apparent that you value the child as an individual, you have opened the door to a successful working relationship.

Carrie's First Session

Here is how Janice handled her first session with Carrie:

Janice: Carrie, I've noticed that sometimes when you read, you have a bit of trouble remembering what words you are reading or how to help yourself figure out some of the words. I'm going to help you work on that. Would that be okay?

[Carrie nods.]

Janice: Let's talk about some of the things you can do when you come to a word you don't know.

Carrie: I can skip it.

Janice: Yes, and then what?

Carrie: Go back and try it again.

Janice: So you would skip the word you don't know and read the rest of the sentence, and then go back to the beginning of the sentence and try again?

Carrie: Yeah, that's what I'd do.

Janice: Can you show me? Let's start this story, and you can show me and tell me what you do.

Janice wanted to see which strategies Carrie felt confident using and which she would need to learn. She wanted Carrie to become conscious of her choices and to become aware that she might need to remind herself which strategy to use — maybe by talking aloud to herself.

Andrew's First Session

Martin's first session with Andrew was very different. Andrew already felt
defeated and needed to be convinced that reading was something he could
do. To help him understand what their respective roles would be, Martin used
the metaphor of coach and player — a relationship that Andrew knew well.

Martin: I'd like to help you with your reading so you will be able to read the
books you like. What do you think?

Andrew: Can you really do that?

Martin: I can try. Do you know what a coach is?

Andrew: Sure. I have a coach for hockey.

Martin: So what does he do?

Andrew: He tells me stuff, like what to do to score. Like, not doing this
[demonstrates] with my wrist and stuff.

Martin: Well, I'm going to be your reading coach. You already know some
things but—like the wrist thing you were telling me about—there are
some things you do that you need to stop doing and some things you
need to start doing. I can show you how. What do you think?

Andrew: Yeah. Okay!

Martin got the first session off to a positive start by committing himself to a
plan of action and eliciting a positive response from Andrew. He hoped that
by using the coach-player image he could help Andrew engage with print in
a more positive manner, giving him the support he needed while
encouraging independence.

The first session sets the stage for a successful teacher-child relationship. It is the first step in establishing rapport with a child. Following are a few guidelines to keep in mind as your partnership grows.

1. Develop a feeling of mutual respect.

- Let the child know that you are there to help and that you value what he or she already knows.
- Let the child know that you are also learning new things and that you will learn from each other.

2. Establish a sense of trust in each other and in the partnership.

- Explain to the child why you will be working together and how your partnership will work.
- Be honest and describe how you think you are going to try to help the child with reading.
- Demonstrate that working with the child is a priority for you by keeping to your schedule. Let the child know this is a commitment that you have made.

3. Create a cooperative relationship.

- Take the time to listen to what the child has to say.
- Engage in conversations about topics that interest the child and about what you are reading together.
- Provide positive feedback and encourage the child's reading attempts without criticism.

4. Be supportive and encouraging.

- Encourage risk-taking, ensuring that the child knows that making miscues and getting mixed up are normal and that you will work together to figure it out.
- Praise the child honestly by pointing out what he or she has done well.
- Make prompts in such a way that the child does not feel they are an interference or criticism but one of the ways you are helping.

5. *Create a learning atmosphere in which the child sees that your partnership and work together is purposeful and has benefits for the child.*

- Establish a sense of purpose for the child by choosing books that he or she will want to read and/or relate to activities and themes of personal interest to the child.
- Respect the child's requests to read books of his or her choice whenever appropriate.
- Encourage the child to share what he or she has been reading and practicing with others — classmates, teachers, parents.
- Whenever possible, make connections between what you are doing in Learner Support sessions and the regular classroom program.

6. *Ensure that the child enjoys the Learner Support sessions.*

- Keep the tone of your sessions light and friendly.
- Laugh together. Talk together. Learn together.

A Typical Learner Support Session

A typical Learner Support session is usually fifteen minutes long and divided into three main parts:

- **Focusing** (approximately three minutes) orients the child to the session and, more specifically, to reading.

- **Revisiting** (approximately six minutes) draws on the knowledge the child already has and on texts he or she has already read.

- **Supported practice** (approximately six minutes) provides more opportunity for strategy-building as the child works with new text or works intensively with a familiar text.

During your sessions, sit beside the child so you both can see the books and other materials. This seating arrangement also encourages the growing sense of partnership.

Focusing

The opening warm-up directs the child's attention to some aspect of word study or to a particular reading strategy, as shown in Carrie's story. Teaching strategies that you might use during this time include:

- reviewing sight words
- introducing or continuing to work on a strategy, such as reading on and rereading
- looking at a particular word family
- working with rhyming words, beginning consonants, and vowel combinations

Revisiting

In the second part of the session, the child moves into actual reading, building on knowledge he or she already has. Activities that occur at this stage include:

- rereading a familiar story (one that has already been practiced)
- discussing a story in process, including locating passages in the text to support the discussion

Supported Practice

Finally, the child reads a new text, at the same time receiving instruction in the use of specific strategies. You and the child go through the book or a portion of it together, making and confirming predictions, reading and discussing the text and illustrations, demonstrating reading strategies, and making personal connections to the text. With experience, you will know the kinds of learning supports the child needs most and can make adjustments that will encourage appropriate strategies most effectively.

When you and a child read together in this way, the interaction and support usually proceed quite naturally. What you do will depend on such factors as the child's:

- use of reading strategies
- experience with the language of the text or its format
- familiarity with the actual text
- confidence in reading

As you proceed, build on what the child already knows and can do, moving him or her toward making decisions about which strategies work best in particular situations. Therefore, you might encourage the child to:

- use the information and meaning already obtained from the text in order to predict what makes sense in the context
- decide when it is necessary to figure out a word and when the word can be skipped, entirely or temporarily
- use picture or visual clues to get at the meaning of the print
- attend to the print details that might help in figuring out unfamiliar words

For beginning readers, draw attention to the print by using a finger to trace beneath each word as it is read, or have the child do so. This encourages the child to attend to the details of printed language and to begin correlating written text and oral reading. It also helps to keep the place in the text while he or she tries out such strategies as looking at picture clues, or reading on and coming back to a word.

Learning to make appropriate prompts and intervening in a naturally supportive manner is a teaching process that develops with time and practice. As the transcripts throughout this book show, the interaction that occurs in Learner Support is natural and evolves out of the text, the child's experiences, and the comments or reading attempts the child makes.

Tammy's First Session

The following transcript gives a picture of how all the different factors come together as the child and teacher work on a text.

Elaine: When I saw this book, Tammy, I thought of you.

Tammy: It looks like it's about shopping.

Elaine: Right. In fact, do you remember what you told me about your shopping trip last week?

Tammy: I said I hate to shop with my little sisters.

Elaine: Well, I don't know why this person hates shopping, but that's the title of this book.

Tammy:
[Reads] I Hate Shopping.

Elaine: That's it exactly. *[Turns to title page.]* Look at her face.

Tammy: She's rolling her eyes.

Elaine: Why do you suppose she's doing that?

Tammy: She knows, that's why.

Elaine: Knows what?

Tammy: Knows what's going to happen—at the shopping—you know.

Elaine: Turn the page and let's see what does happen.

Tammy: That's just like my mom. See, she's talking, and nothing's in the basket. Only by now, my sisters would be into everything!

Elaine: Let's read it and find out what she's thinking.

Tammy:
[Reads] I hate shopping with my mom. She can . . . She ca . . . n . . . can. . .

Elaine: She seems to be looking for something in her purse. What do you think that might be?

Tammy: Her list?

Elaine: So what's her problem?

Tammy: She can't find her list.

Elaine: Try the sentence again and think about how to say that.

Tammy:
[Reads] She can n . . . never f . . . find her list and she can n . . . *[pauses, reads from the beginning of the sentence, stopping at never, and then completes the sentence]* and she can never find the things she wants.

Elaine: I liked the way you noticed the word never had been used earlier in the sentence. You reread it and checked it out. Good for you. Will you try that sentence once more?

Elaine drew upon a conversation they had held earlier, setting the stage for a successful reading by ensuring that Tammy would be able to relate to the experience and to the text. She also acknowledged what Tammy did correctly and brought it to her attention, an important factor in raising Tammy's confidence.

This brief transcript demonstrates that Learner Support works most successfully when teachers have a base of knowledge upon which to draw, an understanding of what experienced readers do, and a willingness to let their own instincts and professional expertise guide them.

CHAPTER 6

Techniques That Support Learning

This chapter describes a number of techniques you can use to help support and teach the students you have selected for help.

Prompting

Prompting is perhaps the most important Learner Support technique, and the most frequently used during strategy sessions. It is a subtle art that requires careful timing and a knowledge of the prompts that are most effective for different situations. Appropriate prompts can be used as stepping-stones to help children decide which problem-solving strategies they need to use, and to help students become aware of the effectiveness of using those strategies.

Prompts can remind children not only to think about how a word, phrase, or segment of text fits into the larger piece of text they are reading, but also to provide feedback and encouragement, and to help them understand what they have read. Prompts develop early independence in readers by helping them to see that there is much they themselves bring to the reading.

Andrew's Story

Recall Andrew's profile. He had a lot of things going for him. He had a good sight vocabulary and a wealth of general knowledge. Yet, when he read, he did not draw on this knowledge base. He relied too heavily on phonics at the expense of fluency and meaning. The prompts his teacher used helped Andrew draw on the knowledge he possessed and directed his attention primarily to the meaning.

This transcript focuses on a reading of *The Knight at Dawn*, by Mary Pope Osborne. The book's text is on the left; Martin's prompts and Andrew's attempts are on the right. The words that Andrew found difficult to read are underlined.

Annie flicked off the light.

Silence.	**Martin:** What she heard.
	Andrew: Sil...sil...ence!
"They aren't moving," Jack whispered.	**Andrew:** Are.
	Martin: It has more on it; it's a contraction and the opposite of are. Try again.
	Martin: The way he is speaking.
Annie turned the light back on. "They're just suits," Jack said.	**Martin:** Suits.
"Without heads," said Annie.	
"Let me have the flashlight a second," said Jack. "So I can look in the book."	**Martin:** What would Jack need to help him see better?
	Martin: Try breaking it into two words.

Annie handed him the flashlight. He pulled out the castle book. He flipped through the pages until he found what he was looking for.

Jack put the book away. "It's called the <u>armory</u>," he said. "It's where armor and weapons are stored."

Martin:	Keep reading to see if it will help.
Martin:	Do you know what this place is called?
Andrew:	Armory.

He shined the flashlight around the room.

"Oh, man," <u>whispered</u> Jack.

Martin:	He is still speaking like this.

The light fell on <u>shiny</u> <u>breastplates</u>, leg plates, arm plates. On shelves filled with helmets and weapons.

Martin:	It describes the way the armor looks when it is polished.
Martin:	Try breaking it into two words again.

<u>On shields, spears, swords,</u>
<u>crossbows, clubs, battle-axes</u>.

There was a <u>noise</u> in the hall.

Martin:	It's a list of all the weapons they saw.
Andrew:	Nose.
Martin:	Does that make sense? No? Then what would?

<u>Voices</u>!

Martin:	What do you think they heard?

"Let's hide!" said Annie.

"<u>Wait</u>," said Jack. "I got to check on something first."

Martin:	Keep reading.
Martin:	So what did he want her to do?

"<u>Hurry</u>," said Annie.

Martin:	They need to get out of there fast, so what does she say?

"It'll take just a second," said Jack. "Hold this." He handed Annie the flashlight.

He tried to lift a helmet from a shelf. It was too heavy. He bent over and dragged the helmet over his head. The <u>visor</u> slammed shut.

Martin: It's the front part of the helmet.

"Oh, forget it." It was <u>worse</u> than having a five-year-old on your head. More like having a ten-year-old on your head.

Martin: He hoped it would help, but now things weren't better, they were . . .

Not only could Jack not lift his head, he couldn't see anything, either.

"Jack!" Annie's voice sounded far away.

Charles's Story

Charles, on the other hand, was an overpredictive reader. He was able to guess his way through most text, often without his eyes on the print. For Charles, attention to the print was the crucial issue. In fact, it was helpful to cover up the picture at times, to redirect his attention to the print.

The following text is from *Rabbit's Birthday Kite*, by Maryann Macdonald.

But Rabbit grabbed the <u>string</u>.

Anna: What's this? *[Writes ing.]* What's this? *[Writes ring.]* What's this? *[Points to string.]*

He began to run. "I have <u>seen</u> kite flying before," he yelled. "It's easy."

Anna: Do you see a word you know?

Charles: See.

Anna: Put the n on it.

Rabbit <u>ran</u> as fast as he could.

Anna: Look again. Do you see a word you know?

Charles: An.

Anna: This rhymes with it.

Charles: Ran.

The kite <u>rose</u> into the air.

Anna: Do you know this word? *[Writes nose.]* This word rhymes with it.

Anna repeatedly asked Charles to focus on the information available from the print. He was using other strategies, but at the expense of the graphophonic information. She needed to coach him in how to use that information as well, when it was appropriate, in the same way that he used his prediction skills.

Sample Prompts

Here are some other examples of prompts that effectively support children in their reading in different situations. The actual prompts you use will depend on the child's confidence and ability to use different strategies, as well as on what you and the child have worked on previously and the text you are now reading.

Prompts really are impromptu suggestions that grow out of the text and the child's ability to make sense of it. Even though prompting soon becomes natural and automatic, you may want to keep a list of some possible prompts and a list of strategies near at hand just to get started.

1. *If a child has made an attempt to figure out the word but has been unsuccessful, value the attempt and follow it up with information or a suggestion that might help the child make a prediction.*

- That's a good try. See if you can find any clue in the picture that might help you.
- I noticed that you used the picture to help you. Try looking at the first sound in the word and see if it helps you find a word in the picture that might fit there.

2. *Try to make a link to a word that was in a book the child has already read or to another story. This kind of prompt encourages the child to draw on previous experiences as a reader and make connections between texts.*

- Rabbit made one of these in the story you read yesterday.
- This part tells about the size of the whale, like the dinosaur book did.

3. *If the child stops at a word and does not seem to know what to do next, encourage him or her to think about some strategies to try. Then experiment with any suggestion the child makes, to see how it works.*

• What do you think we might do to help figure out this word?

This particular kind of prompting is very useful once in a while. Although it interrupts the meaning of the text, it does provide the child with the opportunity to think about different strategies and try them out.

4. *If the child is still unable to figure out a word after several attempts, then you will need to suggest solutions.*

• Let's try leaving it out and moving on this time.
• Try rereading the sentence and taking another run at the word.
• Read on and see if that helps.
• Try skipping the word for now and maybe you will get it after you finish reading the sentence.
• Try using another word that you think might work there.
• Look at the beginning sound of the word and see if that will help you decide what word might make sense.

5. *You may find that some children respond better to visual prompts than to oral ones. (See Reproducible 14, page 85.) Visual prompts can be very effective since they do not interrupt the flow of the text; eventually, you may not need to use oral prompts as often.*

6. *The easiest prompt, but one that shouldn't be overused, is simply telling the child the word.*

Frank Smith (1978) points out that stopping to figure out unfamiliar words interrupts a child's comprehension of what has been read, since the child can hold what he or she has read in short-term memory for only a limited time. So, if a child has taken a lot of time to figure out a word, you need to encourage him or her to go back and reread the sentence to that point. In the end, if the child is unable to continue the reading even with a prompt, then simply supplying the word may be necessary to keep the reading moving along.

Prompts That Discourage Children

It is also important to recognize that some prompts are neither effective nor supportive. These prompts imply criticism of the child's ability to read, even if said in a praising way:

- Oh, come on now, you know this word.
- We learned this word yesterday. You remember, don't you?
- That word was on the last page. I told it to you then.
- Sound it out. You know how to do that.
- That word's not hard. You can figure it out if you try.

Prompts like these put pressure on the child, even though they are cloaked in praise. They make the child feel the need to be able to do something; if he or she cannot do it, such prompts simply become a reminder of the child's difficulty with reading.

Using Prompts Effectively

During support sessions, you need to concentrate on making the student feel good about reading and confident in his or her reading ability. It also helps if you can point out signs of progress. An important goal is helping children to develop a feeling of confidence and to see themselves as readers.

As a child reads a passage of text, it is important to strike a balance between giving sufficient time and opportunity for the child to try and figure the words out alone, and your intervening. Consciously using the "pause, prompt, praise" technique will help establish that balance.

When a child comes to an unfamiliar word, don't jump in to assist too quickly. It may help to count to five slowly before you prompt the child. Praise any attempt, especially if an appropriate strategy or cue has been used, even if it did not result in an accurate reading of the word or phrase.

- Good work. You used the *b* at the beginning of the word to help you figure that out.
- That's almost right. *House* would make sense there, but the author used the word *home* instead.
- Good try, but take another look at the end of the word.
- You're right. When I look at the picture, I can see why you thought the word might be *summer*.
- That's close, but this is a two-part word. Look again and see what the two parts are.

When the child correctly figures out a word, praise should be natural. In most cases, just a nod of the head or a smile that acknowledges the accomplishment is all that you need do.

Other Techniques

Prompting is not the only technique you will find useful. Depending on the child you are working with, you may find one or more of the following effective as well. You may already be using some of them in your regular classroom teaching.

Assisted Reading

This technique helps to evoke interest in a book. Use it to introduce a child to a new book and provide information about the text that can be drawn on when trying to read the book independently.

First, read the selected book — one the child has chosen or one you choose based on your knowledge of the child's interests or reading level or both — strictly for enjoyment. Talk about the cover, the illustrations, the format, what you both think of the book, and so on.

Then read it again, inviting the child to participate in the reading at highly predictable sections of the text, drawing on strong contextual or picture clues, repetitive words or phrases, and/or rhyming words. Do this in such a way that the child develops confidence and feels good about how much he or she already knows about the text and how it works.

During the next reading, encourage the child to read the text alone, supporting his or her attempts by reading along quietly or prompting with such reminders as to notice the beginning sounds of words, to look at the picture clues, or to refer to what has already been read.

Cloze Passages

Cloze passages, used when a child needs practice predicting what comes next in a text, can take a variety of forms, depending on your purpose. They can be long or short; they can be drawn directly from a printed text or be a synopsis of it; they can target words in patterns (such as every fifth word) or specific words (such as adverbs or key words in the story).

First, create a written text with the target words eliminated. You can leave the spaces blank, draw boxes where the words should go, or insert a line on which you, the child, or both can write.

For beginning readers, a good way to do cloze passages is to write down sentences from a familiar story and have the child predict the words that go in each space. You can also use nursery rhymes, skipping-rope rhymes, and favorite stories, or songs to help the child become familiar with the activity.

For older children, you might make a copy of a paragraph or a page of a book that they already know, a poem that is highly predictable, or a section of text that they can read comfortably, for the most part. However, the text you select should require students to use their background knowledge of the story and their knowledge of how language works to make predictions about the missing parts.

If you include the beginning letters or phonemes of some words, and prefixes or suffixes of others, cloze passages can also help draw a child's attention to graphophonic cues.

Constructing Word Families

This task can help a child become aware of similarities between words. Begin by creating a simple word, such as *cat*, either on the chalkboard or with magnetic letters on a magnetic board or a metal bread box. Then ask the child to spell *mat*, *rat*, and so on. Point out the similarities in the words.

After a few such sessions, most children usually begin to see that only one letter needs to be changed in order to make a new word. Repeat this activity as many times as necessary until an understanding is built.

Dictated Sentences

Dictated sentences help a child develop an awareness of the connection between reading and writing. They also provide opportunities for a child to read familiar stories in his or her own words.

After reading a book, ask the child to retell the story or a favorite part of it. Write down what the child says, reading aloud as you go. With a young child, you may want to number the sentences so that later the child can draw illustrations for each one. After you have recorded the child's version of the story, or as much of it as you feel appropriate, ask for an oral rereading. With young readers, it is a good idea to keep the dictated retelling to three or four sentences.

You may have to make decisions regarding how grammatically correct you want the recorded sentences to be. For some children, changing what they say — eliminating the *ain't*s and double negatives, fixing up tenses, and rearranging words — will be confusing as they attempt to reread. You may wish to discuss any changes you think are necessary.

Because children remember what they have said and connect it to what they see written on the paper, this kind of reading helps to make explicit the match between oral and written language and is a stepping stone to reading other kinds of written texts. If the change from what the child actually said is too great, the child may "read" what he or she said, not what you recorded on paper.

Echo Reading

Echo reading provides a fluent oral model for a child and gives an opportunity to practice inflection and intonation. It is especially helpful for a child who tends to read word by word, or who needs practice in running words and phrases together in a natural flow.

In echo reading, you read a sentence of the text and have the child read it back to you. Remind and encourage the child to make the reading sound interesting. You can do echo reading sentence by sentence with early readers, but with older children you may want to model the reading of several sentences or a short paragraph at one time. By reading the piece fluently and smoothly, you demonstrate how the language of the text should flow and give the child a chance to get a feel for it.

Elkonin Boxes

To help a child think about the order of the sounds in spoken words, use an Elkonin box — a picture matrix of a word that contains a box for each phoneme (not letter) of the word.

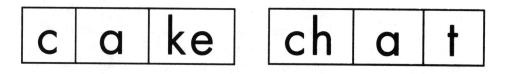

Choose some words from a familiar story and say each one slowly, sound by sound, placing a chip in each section of the Elkonin box for each separate sound you make. Encourage the child to join in on the articulation of the word and, when ready, to be the one to place the chips in the boxes. Eventually the child should be able to answer such questions as:

What is the first sound you hear in . . .?
What sound comes after *a* in *cake*?

You can also use this technique to relate sound segments to letters, or to look at a particular word the child has been asked to spell, either from a piece of writing or from the vocabulary of the story. Draw the appropriate sound boxes and have the child write in as many letters as he or she hears, skipping those sounds that are not recognized.

You may want to include a chalkboard, wipe-off message board, or "magic" slate in the child's Learner Support folder or box for this purpose.

Language Experience

This technique encourages a child to make connections between what is being said and how it is recorded in a written format.

Ask the child to decide on a topic for writing: family, pet, friends, favorite activities or places, something that happened in school. Then tell the child that you are going to be the secretary and write down whatever he or she wants to say.

The method of recording depends on the child and the amount of writing required. With young children, you may want to print the story as dictated; for older children, you might use a computer. The main objective is to record the child's words in a format that allows him or her to see it as printed text. Once the dictation has been completed, have the child read back what you wrote.

Open-Ended Poems and Songs

You can help a child focus on particular strategies or skills by selecting shorter pieces to read. For example, you can use poems or songs that give repeated practice with rhyme in a meaningful context or that lend themselves to the demonstration of a particular strategy, such as reading on or rereading.

Oral Reading by the Teacher

Whenever possible, read aloud to a child who lacks the background experience necessary to get started at reading, or who lacks experience with language structures or vocabulary. This oral reading models the language and story format that a child will need for his or her own later attempts at reading the book. It also provides a demonstration of fluent reading behavior and an enjoyable reading experience.

Paired Reading

When using this technique, you and the child read the book together, with the child taking over when he or she wishes to by using a predetermined signal. Together, you can determine the signal (a tap on the book, touching your arm, raising a finger) beforehand. Once the child has signaled, you stop reading until the child gives another signal. If the reading is bogging down, begin reading as you feel appropriate.

Phonemic Segmentation

Phonemic segmentation helps a child to become aware that spoken words contain separate segments (phonemes) and to recognize that the same phonemes occur in different words.

Here are two games you can use to encourage a child to distinguish sounds in words. The first is a variation of I Spy. In this version children look for words that begin or end with particular phonemes. For example:

- I spy with my little eye, something that begins with the *m* sound.
- I spy with my little eye, something that ends with the *t* sound.

In the second game, called Sausages, you start by saying a word, and the child responds with a word that starts with the last sound of yours. You can build the chain of words on a magnetic board. For example: *chalk . . . kites . . . sandwich . . . chair . . . ruler.*

Playing with Language

Invite the child to tell you a familiar tongue twister. Write the twister down in large print so he or she can see the connections between the spoken words and the words on paper.

Use word games in which you physically move words around to create sentences, as you do with sentence boards. For a variation of Scrabble, you might print a different word on each of the six sides of several wooden cubes. Have the child take turns with you rolling the cubes and trying to make sentences using the words that turn face up. A child can also gain experience with words by using felt and magnetic letters to make up sentences.

By encouraging children to have fun playing with letters and words, you provide a nonthreatening way for them to become more familiar with how letters and words go together to make spoken or written language.

Rebus Stories

A rebus story can remind a child that using picture cues can be an effective reading strategy. It also provides a tool for reading a passage of text fluently. Because these stories replace potentially troublesome words with appropriate pictures, a child can quickly gain confidence in his or her ability to read new pieces of text.

Some trade books have stories told in the rebus format. You can also use activity books with rebus stories and puzzles. An easy way to make a rebus story is to copy a printed text, blank out certain words, and draw pictures to replace the words.

You can also create individual prompt cards for any book and use a pocket chart. On one side of each card place a picture, with the corresponding word printed on the other side. As you read the story with the child, show the prompt cards as necessary, turning them over after the child gives the words from the picture cues so that he or she can see those words in written form. After reading all of the text, reread the passage using the word side of the cards, flipping back to the pictures for reference only as required.

Responsive Reading

Once a child is familiar with the pattern of a repetitive text you are reading aloud, he or she can join in to read the repeated parts. This strategy is a good stepping-stone for children who are hesitant about trying to read, offering them a chance to try out their reading voice.

Rhyme and Alliteration Games

These kinds of word games provide a child with the opportunity to play with language and gain an awareness of how words fall into certain patterns of sounds.

Riddle Games

When you give a child a riddle to figure out, include in your clues hints about rhymes or similar sound patterns. For example:

- I'm thinking of a word that starts like *house* and likes to gallop across fields.
- I'm thinking of a word that rhymes with *rat*, sits on my head, and keeps the sun out of my eyes.

Sentence Boards

Sentence boards are an excellent tool for the practice of individual sight words. They also demonstrate how words go together to make meaningful sentences and text.

Either purchase or make word cards with individual words on them. These should include a good assortment of basic sight words as well as words that will be meaningful to the child you are working with, either from personal experience or from pieces of familiar text. Even better, have the child help you make the word cards. Invite the child to suggest names of people and pets, places they go, things they like to do, and so on. You can also write words from stories and books he or she is reading.

Together arrange the words in sentences. Do this on a table, or use a sentence board (a stiff piece of material with plastic see-through pockets into which the words are inserted horizontally), or a large pocket chart. The physical act of moving the words and then trying to read the sentences provides the child with the added experience of seeing how language works, how words go together, what makes sense, and what does not.

Sight Words

Many children in Learner Support still need to build a basic sight-word vocabulary. The "bedrock sight vocabulary" listed by Holdaway (1980, pages 145–156) provides both a means of assessing a child's sight vocabulary and a method of helping to extend it. Holdaway suggests writing the words on cards, one word to each card, with a contextual sentence on the back. Although sentences are included with his original list, it will be better to invite the child to think of and dictate a sentence as you write it on the card.

To help the child practice a word, show the word side first. If he or she is unable to recognize the word out of context, turn the card over and see if the sentence helps. This provides an opportunity for the child to recall the word from memory but, if the recall is unsuccessful, immediately adds clues and connections to help figure out the word and recall it in the future. Even if the child recalls the word from memory, turning the card over to read the sentence will confirm his or her success — a confidence booster as well as a bit of extra practice in reading the word in context.

Story Writing

This technique provides a student with an opportunity to use his or her imagination and knowledge of how language works to write stories, poems, and songs. It allows a child to incorporate patterns of language — repetitive phrases, rhyme, familiar book patterns — and favorite story lines and characters into pieces of writing that can be used later as texts for reading.

You can modify story writing to meet individual needs, interests, and abilities. For very young children, you may want to serve as secretary to record their ideas. Begin by inviting the child to write a story with you. Together, decide what the story will be about. Ideas can come from a picture or a piece of writing you noticed the child working on during regular class time or from a book you have read together. If you have read a book with a particular pattern, for example, or one with characters or events that especially interested the child, this might be a good starting place. As you record the child's ideas, work with him or her until the writing makes sense. Once again, you will have to decide on the appropriate balance between proper grammar and the child's own words.

Your assistance to older children in the recording of their stories might be in helping them to clarify their ideas. Explain that, since these pieces of writing may be used as reading material for future sessions, you will "edit" the piece after it is completed. It is especially effective to give the pieces a finished, professional look by writing them on the computer. Seeing themselves as published authors gives children a real boost.

Since this kind of writing takes more time than Learner Support sessions allow for on a regular basis, you may want to use this technique only with those children whose own writing is the best possible text to work with. Some children engage with their own texts much more readily than with any other. Because they are reading their own ideas, their reading is supported by familiarity and personal connections that encourage engagement and facilitate their attempts to make sense of the text — an important first step on the road to learning to read. Reading their own words also demonstrates to children that their thoughts and ideas are valued and worthy to be shared with others. The resulting rise in self-esteem can have far-reaching effects as children begin to see themselves as readers and writers.

Strategy Picture Cards

Some children respond better to visual cues than to oral prompts. Strategy picture cards provide a visual method of prompting a child who is reading aloud to you.

You can either use the strategy picture cards in Reproducible 14 on page 85 or create your own graphics with a child. Put each one on a separate file card and lay the cards on a table. If a prompt becomes necessary, point to the appropriate strategy card as you prompt verbally. Gradually reducing the number of verbal prompts will help move the child toward independent reading and away from dependence on you for help.

14. Strategy Picture Cards

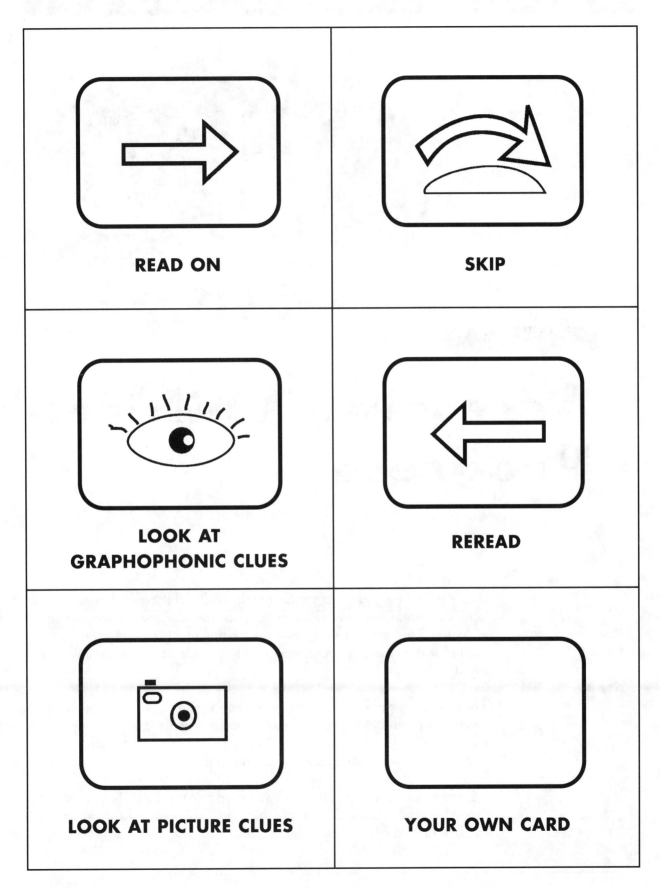

READ ON

SKIP

LOOK AT
GRAPHOPHONIC CLUES

REREAD

LOOK AT PICTURE CLUES

YOUR OWN CARD

CHAPTER 7

Assessing Children's Progress

By the time you begin working with specific children in Learner Support sessions, you will already have a baseline profile of those children as readers. This information gives you a starting point from which to document their learning progress, as well as provide a basis for establishing appropriate goals.

The goals for a child's learning must be realistic and flexible. As you work together, a picture will unfold of how the child is doing at any given point. At the same time, you will want to look ahead and consider the strategies that you need to introduce, reinforce, and practice.

It is important to keep in mind that you need to consistently be patient, supportive, and realistic. Remember that things come more easily to some children than to others. Some children might try a strategy only a few times before they feel comfortable with it — skipping over a difficult word, going back to the beginning of the sentence and taking another run at it, and so on. After a few prompts and reminders, these children use one or more appropriate strategies quite readily. For a variety of reasons, however, other children take a long time and require a great deal of continued support and coaching before they begin to try out strategies without being prompted.

> After a few months working with Carrie, I began getting anxious to show bigger results. I started to get impatient. I thought I had to move Carrie along more quickly.
>
> So I started putting on the pressure during sessions, and I let Carrie see my impatience. She began to struggle even more. She seemed to have more days where she struggled to remember what she already knew. Carrie seemed to be regressing, not progressing.
>
> After a few sessions, I asked our Resource teacher to come and observe, to give me some feedback on what was going on. She said she thought I was in a hurry. As we talked I realized I was not on any fixed schedule here. When I became more relaxed, so did Carrie, and I was a much better coach.
>
> **—Janice, grade 4 teacher**

Informal Assessment Measures

Children demonstrate their progress in different ways. For some children, progress is orderly and immediately apparent as they try out certain strategies, find out when and how they work, and use them independently. For others, progress is slow and arduous, developing out of many sessions and supported by positive reinforcement and encouragement in the classroom over a long period of time. The rate at which a child grows and develops as a reader is as individual in nature as each child's personality, background experience, and abilities. However, all children will show evidence of growth if you know what to look for.

The key to whatever informal assessment you do is that it should not require a lot of time or energy. Its purpose is chiefly to help you keep tabs on how the child is doing and how you are doing in helping the child. Informal assessment provides an up-to-date evaluation of the child's progress and helps you make decisions about the best kind of support to offer in the future. At the same time, it gives you an ongoing record to discuss with families and with other educators who support the child outside the classroom.

Observing and Recording

The most evident signs of progress are usually found in the child's reading behavior. You are seeing progress when a child:

- tries using a strategy without being prompted
- makes a connection between similar words or books or writing styles
- remembers a strategy used in a similar situation and tries it again
- fluently reads a book he or she has been working on

For some children, one-on-one assistance and support may be all that's needed to encourage rapid — at times, almost surprising — progress. Children thrive on a regularly scheduled opportunity to have feedback on their reading. It is all that many of them need to work through a problem period or to get the idea of how to use one or more strategies in an effective manner. For these children, the signs of progress are clearly visible. They begin using strategies effectively, they feel sufficiently confident to use them independently, and their reading improves by leaps and bounds.

Slower progress for a child may be caused by:

- the nature of the reading difficulty the child is experiencing
- the child's level of confidence about reading
- the child's poor self-image as a reader
- a combination of these factors

A child who lacks confidence may have reached a stage where reading is so frustrating and unrewarding that it is perceived as something that the child "can't do," or that is "too hard." For these children, much of the work in the early sessions focuses on building self-confidence and developing a more positive attitude toward reading. This can be a long, slow process requiring a great deal of patience.

Signs of growth also reveal themselves outside the Learner Support sessions. Some children who avoided reading and associated activities beforehand now:

- ask when the next session is
- remind you about a new book they want to read
- are eager to tell you about any books they receive as gifts
- enthusiastically share what happens in a story they have read or written themselves

No sign of progress is more rewarding than the positive feedback that comes from family members. In some cases, if a child has had reading difficulties for some time, the family may initially be skeptical that Learner Support will help, and they are delighted to see the child's developing abilities and confidence. When parents of children who have been experiencing reading difficulties for a long time tell you that they are amazed at what their children can do, or say things like, "My child is doing more than I would have ever thought possible before," you know that the extra help is working.

Taking Stock

It is important to take time periodically to reflect on how the sessions are going and how each child is progressing. Reproducible 15 offers one assessment format for your own use.

Formal Assessment Measures

Periodically, you might want to use forms, such as Reproducibles 16 and 17, to provide a more formal record of each child's reading development. With some children you may find it useful to take a running record once a week, as well as use miscue analysis and cloze passages now and then. These measures will provide you with a visible record of the child's progress and reveal patterns and needs.

15. Taking Stock: Teacher's Assessment

Name _____ Date _____

Teacher's Name _____

1   How do I feel the child is progressing? What evidence do I see of this?

2   How do I feel about what is happening in our Learner Support sessions?

3   What strategies is the child now using successfully?

4   What does the child need to continue working on?

5   How does the child now feel about reading?

6   How does the child feel about Learner Support?

7   How can I continue to support the child's learning?

8   What could I do or how could I modify what we are doing to help the child more in future sessions?

9   Where do we go from here?

16. Profile of the Early Reader

Name _____ Date _____

The Early Reader	Comments
Rereads miscues that disturb meaning.	
Predicts outcomes of stories from pictures in the text.	
Recalls events of stories in logical sequence.	
Discusses and retells stories.	
Realizes print can be read.	
Knows that what is said can be written.	
Names *letter*, *word*, *sound* appropriately.	
Knows print goes from left to right in English.	
Reads pages in correct sequence.	
Locates individual letters.	
Chooses books for free time.	
Demonstrates awareness of book language.	
Makes eye/ear/voice matches.	
Makes predictions that are grammatically appropriate.	
Rereads miscues that do not disturb meaning.	
Distinguishes beginning, middle, final sounds.	

CHAPTER 8

Informing and Involving Families

Effective communication is important in any family-teacher relationship, but it plays a particularly important role in Learner Support. Good communication ensures that the school and home work together in the best interest of the child, and that any concerns and questions arising on either side are dealt with quickly and effectively.

The families of children who have experienced reading difficulties for some time may have developed negative attitudes or frustrations regarding their child's ability to learn to read. Some may be thankful for any help that is available, while others may no longer expect much progress to be made.

Because Learner Support is part of the regular classroom structure and program, it is technically not necessary to obtain a family's approval and support. Just the same, it often adds to a child's success if you let the parents know how Learner Support works, why it is being offered to their child, and how they can extend the child's literacy learning into the home. If possible, share your information in a face-to-face meeting with the family, but if that is not feasible, a letter or phone call will work.

As you talk to families, you may want to discuss how all children learn to read and what conditions can enhance that learning. Reproducibles 18, 19, and 20 on pages 95-97 provide you with a brochure you can give or send to families explaining how they can help their child. To make the brochure, fold a piece of 8 1/2" x 11" paper in half. Copy (reducing by 50%) Reproducible 18 onto the first page and Reproducibles 19 and 20 onto the two center pages respectively. You may wish to add a personal note on the last page.

When meeting with parents, you might want to:

- Remind them how their children learned to do many things at home before they came to school.
- Stress how important parents are as teachers and models.
- Reassure them that this role continues after their children come to school.
- Explain the need for families and teachers to work together as partners in a child's learning. (You will find more information about this topic in Doake, 1988 and Baskwill, 1989.)
- Explain how Learner Support is set up and what goals you hope to achieve.

After the initial contact, keep families informed through conversations and the pass-along book. Write notes not only about the big accomplishments but also about what happens day to day or week to week. Properly used, the pass-along book does more than give parents information about their child; it provides tips and ideas for encouraging the child to read at home as well.

Periodically, you will also want to report to families in a more official "report card" way, not only to share the information but also to reinforce the idea that Learner Support is a regular part of the child's participation in your classroom program. One thing to keep in mind is that each family is quite different. Your reports should meet the specific needs and expectations of each family as much as possible.

Guiding the Family

If you decide to send books home, be sure they are ones the child has worked on and is able to read quite fluently. Encourage parents to be positive about their child's reading by applauding his or her reading efforts, recognizing that learning is going on, and not worrying about the "mistakes" or "miscues" the child might make while reading.

Refocusing Family Support

Support from families comes in different forms. Some parents have specific ideas about how reading should be taught, generally based on their own experiences as students, or on the experiences of other children in the family. Many will also be very conscious of discussions in the media of the value of a particular type of instruction. Some families may still have difficulty encouraging their children in a positive way. This is especially true when they fear that the child might not overcome his or her reading difficulties — a fear that usually results in extreme pressure for both the parent and the child.

When children experience difficulties in school, their parents may find it difficult to deal with their fears about the future. Just as children's self-esteem is diminished if they are unable to read as well as their peers do, so too does the self-esteem of family members drop when their children are not doing as well as others. The whole process becomes cyclical, usually with the result that neither the child nor the parent feels good about the child's schooling or future. Expectations may lower, a sense of despair and frustration may set in, and blame may be directed at any available person or institution.

If a parent's involvement interferes with work at school, or is negative or punitive in nature, it may be in the best interest of the child to treat reading at home as one type of reading and reading independently or at school as a different type. It is up to you to consider what is best for the child and make the necessary decisions based on your knowledge and understanding of the situation.

18. About Reading

Dear Parent or Caregiver,

For many children, learning to read is like putting together a puzzle. Here are some ways you can help your child put this puzzle together.

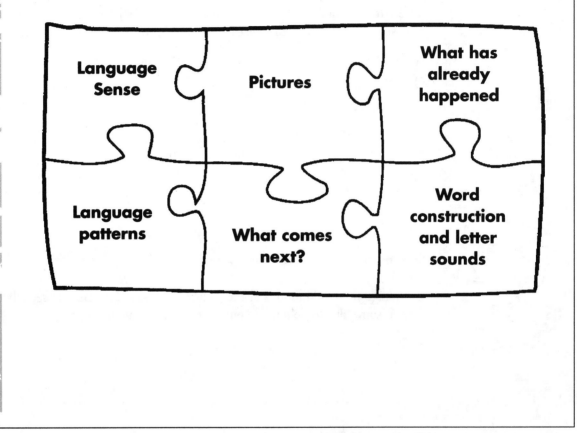

19. About Reading

1. *Language Sense*

Knowledge of how words, phrases, and sentences work together

From birth, children learn about language through conversations at home, playing with friends, listening to the radio, watching television, and so on. As a result, children grow up knowing how words name things, describe things, denote action, and link thoughts. Children also learn how language has different tones and sounds, how words can ask questions, and how words can represent thoughts. Children learn how words go together to make sense.

As your child reads aloud, you can encourage use of this "language sense" by asking questions such as:

- Did that sound right?
- Does that make sense?
- What do you think would make sense there?

2. *Pictures*

Information in pictures and graphics

Encourage your child to look at the pictures, maps, and graphics to see whether there is some clue to help figure out what might come next in the text.

- Can you find something to give you a clue?
- What does the picture show?

3. *What Has Already Happened*

What has already been read

Just as oral language makes sense, so does printed language. When a child reads, keeping in mind what has already happened can give important clues about what might happen next or what the text says. Ask questions such as:

- What do you think might happen next?
- What happened when . . .
- Do you remember the part we read about . . .

20. About Reading

4. *Language Patterns*

Language patterns in the text

Certain kinds of text include patterns that can help a reader. These patterns include:

- patterns of words, phrases, or verses that repeat such as
   Teddy Bear, Teddy Bear
- rhyming words such as
   One, two, buckle my shoe
- flowing rhythms such as
   Over in the meadow
   where the green grass grows

Look for such patterns in nursery rhymes, poems, songs, and stories. As your child reads with you, point out these patterns so he or she can use them to help figure out the text.

5. *What Comes Next*

Words that come after unknown words

Sometimes skipping a word can help determine an unknown word. This is called *reading on*. Encourage your child to read beyond a problem word to see if that will help give a needed clue. Then ask your child to go back to the start of the sentence and try again.

6. *Word Construction and Letter Sounds*

The letter sounds of the words in the text

When other strategies fail, encourage your child to look at the letters and combinations of letters in the word. Looking at the first letter sound and/or familiar word parts (beginnings, endings, root words, etc.) can provide another important piece of the puzzle.

fish, fishing   walked, talked   slow, slowly, slowest

Good readers learn to put all the pieces of the reading puzzle together. Learning how to do this requires lots of practice. Encourage your child to try what he or she thinks will work and to try something else if that piece of the puzzle doesn't fit.

Enjoy your shared reading times. Together, you and your child can make a great reading team!

CHAPTER 9

Organizing For Learner Support

Before you begin to implement Learner Support, you must decide how to carry it out with as little disruption as possible to the daily running of the classroom and to the work and routines of the other children. In most cases, once the planning and organization are in place and you have found an efficient method of making the sessions a natural extension of your existing classroom activities, Learner Support will run smoothly with little additional effort on your part.

Organizing the Other Children

The first question that may come to your mind is: "What do I do with the other students while I am working with one child?" In order for you to focus your attention during the Learner Support sessions, the rest of the class needs to be engaged in productive independent work. You must be confident that they too are involved in learning that is not only engaging, but also challenging and effective.

You may already have scheduled times when students work independently. Scheduled activities, such as personal reading, sustained silent reading, personal writing, independent practice, independent activity time, theme work, center activities, project work, library sessions, or research activity can provide blocks of time for individual Learner Support sessions. The crucial common element for this independent time, however, is that all of the children are involved in activities that engage them productively without your help for at least fifteen minutes at a time.

Organizing Time

> "When I first heard about Learner Support I thought it sounded great, but I really wondered where I would ever get the time to do it. I could not imagine where the time was going to come from. It wasn't as if I had a half hour of free classes each day. I must admit it really boggled the mind at first, but once I got going, it just became a regular part of the daily schedule.
>
> **—Kenneth, grade 1 teacher**

Time is always a factor when you are adding something new to your classroom activities. The biggest part of the job, however, is in figuring out where your sessions will fit into your daily schedule. Look through your schedule, find times when children are working independently for at least fifteen minutes, and schedule in your sessions. Some things to keep in mind are:

1. START OUT SLOWLY.

Begin by taking only one or two children for Learner Support when you are getting started. Schedule at least two sessions per week per child. You can always add more sessions and children as you go along.

2. KEEP SESSIONS TO FIFTEEN MINUTES.

Plan out your sessions, keeping in mind the three parts of each session, and stick to the scheduled fifteen minutes. If sessions become too long, they can drag and become less productive. This means you need to be organized so you can use the full amount of time. Keeping to this schedule will also ensure you the opportunity to get around to the other students quite often as well.

3. MAKE THE COMMITMENT.

Once you begin Learner Support, make it an ongoing priority. Talk to your class and explain that at these times of the day you will be working one-on-one with students and need everyone's cooperation. Make Learner Support sessions a written-in part of your daily plan — no ifs, ands, or buts.

Organizing Materials

Keep a reading folder or box for each child, so you have everything for strategy sessions readily accessible. You can make folders such as the one shown here or cover empty boxes to hold materials.

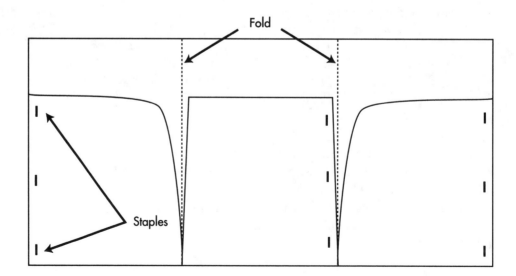

The basic materials to keep in the folder or box include:

Teacher's Diary: a notebook, or separate loose-leaf pages for you to write down notes about each session. The diary should identify the books the child has worked on, the strategies he or she is employing, and what you plan to do at the next session.

Reading Log: a sheet or log in which to record the books the child has read in the Learner Support sessions.

Books: a selection of reading materials/books you have worked on in previous sessions, ones you are presently working on, and a number of new ones from which to select for future sessions.

Strategy Materials: resource materials to help the child work on particular strategies. Items such as sight-word cards, rebus puzzles, sentence strips, visual strategy cards, and cloze passages are just some of the things you might store in the folder or box.

Writing Tools: pen, pencil, and eraser

Organizing Space

The space you'll use for Learner Support sessions takes careful consideration. Find a place where you can meet with the children and furnish it with:

- a student-sized tabletop or desk and two chairs so you and the child can sit side by side
- nearby shelving

Keep the following items on the shelves:

- the children's Learner Support folders or boxes
- other books and/or sets of books used for Learner Support
- pass-along books
- professional books and resources
- spare recording sheets, black-line masters
- writing paper, blank banks, filing cards, sentence strips
- writing implements such as pens, pencils, markers, crayons
- paper clips, stapler and scissors
- word cards, letter disks, word games

The following diagrams illustrate two classrooms with a Learner Support corner. Such designated areas save time, provide an efficient way of organizing materials, and establish a private work space.

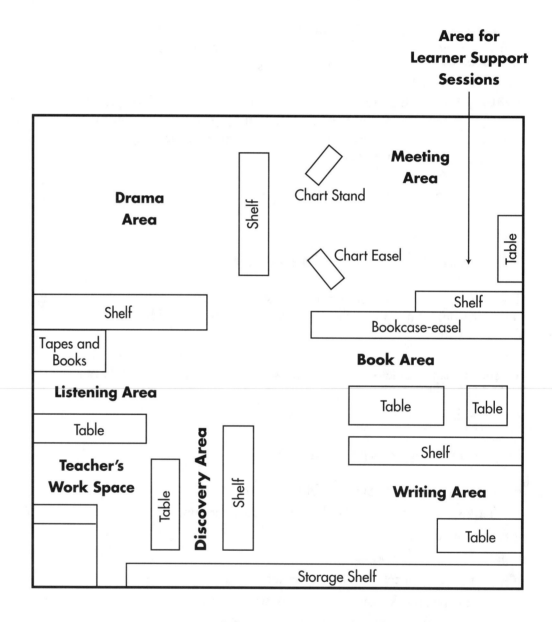

Remember, too, that strategy sessions can be mobile, shifting from place to place if necessary. If you cannot set your classroom up in a similar way, simply make the best use of the space you have available. All that is really needed for successful Learner Support sessions is the teacher, the child, and some books.

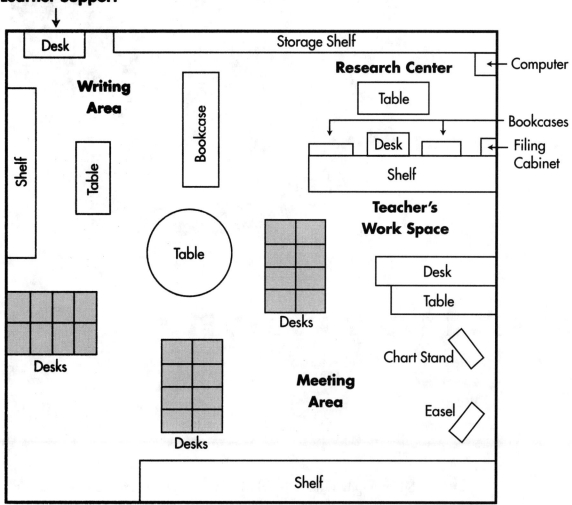

Used for Learner Support

Desk

Storage Shelf

Computer

Research Center

Table

Writing Area

Bookcase

Bookcases

Desk

Filing Cabinet

Shelf

Shelf

Table

Teacher's Work Space

Table

Desk

Table

Desks

Desks

Chart Stand

Meeting Area

Easel

Desks

Shelf

Bibliography

This bibliography is not all-inclusive, or in any way exclusive. Instead, it simply provides a sampling of quality materials now on the market in the selected categories.

Children's Books

Sets and Collections

All Aboard Reading. New York: Grosset & Dunlap. Three-level reading set (preschool to grade 3).

Book Bank. Distributed in Canada by Scholastic Canada and in the United States by the Wright Group. Collections of books for beginning readers. Includes both fiction and nonfiction titles. Incorporates illustrations, repetitive text, and use of rhythm and rhyme to encourage use of a balance of strategies.

Bright and Early Books for Beginning Readers. New York and Toronto: Random House. A well-known collection of books with rhythm, rhyme, and humor.

Early Bird. Scarborough, ON: Nelson, Canada, and Albany, NY: Delmar Publishers. A collection of books for children in junior kindergarten and grade 1, grouped according to accessible themes for children at these levels.

First Stepping Stone Books. New York and Toronto: Random House. A collection of books for beginning readers ready to try longer, less predictable texts. Short chapters with high-interest stories will capture young readers' attention. Series of books with recurring characters.

Golden Readers. Racine, WI and Cambridge, ON: Western Publishing Company. A series of books spanning three reading levels. Stories feature bright illustrations, repetitive use of phrases and words, and short sentences.

Hello Reader! New York and Toronto: Scholastic. Colorful, engaging books encourage children to use a balance of reading strategies. For kindergarten to grade 3. The level D books are appropriate as first chapter books.

I Can Read Books. New York and Toronto: HarperCollins. A large collection of trade books for beginning readers that includes mysteries, adventure stories, poetry, historical fiction, and humor.

Ladybird Books "Read It Yourself" Collection. Lewiston, ME: Ladybird Books. Distributed in Canada and the United States by Penguin. Easy-to-read versions of well-known stories and fairy tales. Recommended for beginning readers to age seven. Ladybird also has the Puddle Lane Collection of early readers that offer delightful stories with colorful illustrations.

Literacy 2000. Distributed in the United States by Rigby. Eight stages, each grouped into the following themes: traditional tales; poems, songs, and rhymes; contemporary stories; science; nonfiction; read-alongs; stories and tales; and rhymes.

Shooting Star. Toronto and New York: Scholastic. A set of first novels for children making the transition from picture books to chapter books.

Step into Reading. New York and Toronto: Random House. A large collection of books divided into four steps or reading levels. Originally intended for parent use.

Stepping Stone Books. New York and Toronto: Random House. A collection of beginning chapter books with high-interest stories.

Step-Up Paperback Books. New York and Toronto: Random House. Two collections of books, Step-Up Nature Books and Step-Up Biographies.

Story Box. Distributed in Canada by Ginn and in the United States by the Wright Group. A multilevel reading series including small books for individual readers and large books to be used with groups of children.

Sunshine Books. Distributed in Canada by Ginn and in the United States by the Wright Group. A five-level collection, including newly introduced sets of science books with graphic supports: diagrams, charts, and photographs.

TWiG Read-Togethers. Distributed in the United States by the Wright Group. This set of books covers four stages for early readers.

Wonder World. Distributed in the United States by the Wright Group. Mostly nonfiction books with predictable structures, rhyme, repetition, and natural language.

Series

The Bobbsey Twins and **The New Bobbsey Twins.** Laura Lee Hope. New York: Simon & Schuster Minstrel Books. Familiar characters.

Boxcar Children. Gertrude Chandler Warner. New York and Toronto: Scholastic. Mystery novels for children in grade 4 and up.

Eagle-Eye Ernie. Susan Pearson. New York: Simon & Schuster Books for Young Readers. A series of beginning chapter books.

Encyclopedia Brown and other books. Donald J. Sobol. New York: Scholastic.

The Kids of the Polk Street School. Patricia Reilly Giff. New York and Toronto: Dell Yearling. A series of books about the adventures of a group of young children. Related series include: New Kids of the Polk Street School, Polka Dot Private Eye, Casey Valentine, and Abby Jones, Junior Detective.

Nate the Great. Marjorie Weinman Sharmat. New York and Toronto: Dell Yearling. Beginning chapter books about a young detective.

The Nic-Nacs and the Nic-Nac News. Joan Lowery Nixon. New York and Toronto: Dell Yearling. Beginning chapter books about a group of young reporters.

Pee Wee Scouts. Judy Delton. New York and Toronto: Dell Young Yearling. Beginning chapter books about children's adventures while working toward earning Pee Wee Scouts badges.

Pinky and Rex. James Howe. New York and Toronto: Macmillan-Atheneum. A series of beginning chapter books about two second-grade children.

Something Queer. Elizabeth Levy. New York and Toronto: Dell Yearling. Graphics and unusual illustrative techniques that capture the interest of most young readers.

Songs to Read. Raffi. New York: Crown Books for Young Readers. Lyrics of well-known children's songs, along with colorful illustrations and a melody line of music.

Books with Specific Characteristics

Picture Books with Little Text

The Cave, Carol Krueger, Book Bank.
Cookies, Rebel Williams, TWiG Read-Togethers.
Fruit Salad, Helen Depree, Wonder World.
Goodnight, Moon, Margaret Wise Brown, Scholastic.
I Can Paint, Helen Depree, Book Bank.
Just Look at You!, Jillian Cutting, Sunshine.
Mud, Wendy Cheyette Lewison, Picture Back Reader, Random House.
The Picnic, Helen Depree, Book Bank.
There's No Place Like Home, Marc Brown, Parents Magazine Press.

Predictable Books with Repetitive Phrases or Patterns

Brown Bear, Brown Bear, Bill Martin, Jr., Scholastic.
Caps for Sale, Esphyr Solbodkina, Scholastic.
The Carrot Seed, Ruth Krauss, Scholastic.
The Fat Cat, Jack Kent, Scholastic.
Have You Seen My Cat?, Eric Carle, Scholastic.
I Was Walking Down the Road, Ann McGovern, Scholastic.
I'm too small. YOU'RE TOO TALL., Judi Barrett, Scholastic.
Oh, Jump in a Sack, Joy Cowley, Story Box.
One Monday Morning, Uri Shulevitz, Scholastic.
Stone Soup, Ann McGovern, Scholastic.
What a Mess, Joy Cowley, Story Box.

Books with Large-Print Text and Fewer Pictures

Arthur's Nose, Marc Brown, Avon Camelot.
Bats: Creatures of the Night, Joyce Milton, All Aboard Reading.
The Big Block of Chocolate, Janet Slater Redhead, Scholastic.
The Big Hug, The Jungle House, John Grace House, Ladybird Books.
Bread and Honey, Frank Asch, Parents Magazine Press.
A Clean House for Mole and Mouse, Harriet Ziefert, Scholastic.
Dancing with Manatees, Faith McNulty, Scholastic.
The Jacket I Wear in the Snow, Shirley Neitzel, Scholastic.
Jennifer Pockets, Jan McPherson, Book Bank.
Leo and Emily's Zoo, Franz Brandenberg, Dell Yearling.
Pickled Peppers, Nancy McArthur, Scholastic.
Rabbit's Birthday Kite, Maryann MacDonald, Bantam.
So Hungry, Harriet Ziefert and Carol Nicklaus, Step into Reading.
The Stone Doll of Sister Brute, Russell Hoban, Dell Yearling.
The Treasure of the Lost Lagoon, Geoffrey Hayes, Step into Reading.
Where's Sylvester's Bed?, JoAnn Balasek, Wonder World.
Why Can't I Fly? Rita Golden Gelman, Scholastic.

Beginning Chapter Books and Short Novels

The Big Sneeze, William Van Horn, Scholastic.
The Bogeyman Caper, Susan Pearson, Simon & Schuster Books for Young Readers.
The Boy with the Helium Head, Phyliss Reynolds Naylor, Dell Yearling.
Camp Big Paw, Doug Cushman, I Can Read Books.
The Case of the Hungry Stranger, Crosby Bonsall, I Can Read Books.
The Clue at the Zoo, Patricia Reilly Giff, Dell Yearling.
Commander Toad and the Space Pirates, Jane Yolen, Break of Day Books, Coward-McCann.
Goldsworthy and Mort in Valentines and Easter Eggs, Marcia Vaughn, HarperCollins.
A Grain of Rice, Helena Clare Pittman, Bantam Skylark.
Hippo Lemonade, Mike Thaler, I Can Read Books.
Horrible Harry's Secret, Suzy Kline, Scholastic.
Nate the Great and *Nate the Great and the Phony Clue*, Marjorie Weinman Sharmat, Dell Yearling.
Owl at Home, Arnold Lobel, Scholastic.
Pinky and Rex and the Mean Old Witch, James Howe, Macmillan-Atheneum.
Revenge of the Bubblegum Monster, Marilyn D. Anderson, Willowisp.

Chapter Books

The Daring Rescue of Marlon the Swimming Pig, Susan Saunders, Stepping Stone Books.
Dragons Don't Read Books, Brenda Bellingham, Shooting Star.

Eliza the Hypnotizer, Michele Granger, Scholastic.
Gorillas, Patricia Demuth, Grosset & Dunlap.
The Great Shamrock Disaster, Patricia Reilly Giff, Dell.
The Knight at Dawn, Mary Pope Osborne, First Stepping Stone Books.
Monsters in the School, Martyn Godfrey, Shooting Star.
Mummies in the Morning, Mary Pope Osborne, First Stepping Stone Books.
The Never Sink Nine in Slugger Mike, Gibbs Davis, Bantam Skylark.
Pet-Sitters Plus Five, Tricia Springstubb, Scholastic.
Secret Land of the Past, Miriam Schlein, Scholastic.
Speedy Sam, Dorothy Joan Harris, Shooting Star.
Trapped in Time, Ruth Chew, Scholastic.

Concept Books

Caught in the Rain, Beatriz Ferro, Early Bird.
An Egg Is to Sit On, Christine Tanz, Early Bird.
How to Cook Scones, Bronwen Scarffe, Bookshelf.
Pairs at the Pool, Ginn Extension Materials, Ginn.
The Rain and the Sun, Alan Trussell-Cullen, Wonder World.
The Seed, Kazuko Nakazawa, Early Bird.
What Season Is This?, Robin Workman, Scholastic.
Wheels, David Lowe, Literacy 2000.

Books with Illustrations that Provide Clues

Arthur's Nose, Marc Brown, Avon Camelot.
Birthdays, Joy Cowley, Sunshine.
A Color of His Own, Leo Lionni, Early Bird.
Come Out and Play, Little Mouse, Robert Kraus, Scholastic.
Fruit Salad, Helen Depree, Wonder World.
Go, Dog, Go!, P.D. Eastman, Beginner Books, Random House.
It Didn't Frighten Me, Janet Goss & Jerome C. Harste, Bookshelf.
The Little Red Hen, Lucinda McQueen, Scholastic.
Lunch Boxes, Fred Ehrlich, Easy-To-Read.
Poor Old Polly, June Melser & Joy Cowley, Story Box.
The Storm, Jackie Goodyear, Literacy 2000.
Would you rather..., John Burningham, Fontana Picture Lions, Collins.
The Zoo, Christine Young, Wonder World.

Question and Answer Format Books

How Do You Make a Bubble?, William J. Hooks, Joanne Oppenheim and
Barbara Brenner, Bank Street.
The Present, Jenny Hessell, Literacy 2000.
Tails, Marcia Vaughn, Bookshelf.
Tails and Claws, Helen Depree, Wonder World.
What Am I?, Brian and Jillian Cutting, Sunshine.

What Do I See in the Garden?, Helen Depree, Wonder World.
What Is This Skeleton?, Brian and Jillian Cutting, Sunshine.
What Would You Like? Joy Cowley, Sunshine.
Where Is Nancy? Virginia King, Literacy 2000.
Whose Toes and Nose Are These?, Marcia Vaughn, Bookshelf.

Books That Are Based on Common Experiences

Bath Time, Sandra Iversen, Wonder World.
The Best Place, Jennifer Beck, Literacy 2000.
Don't Panic, Helen Depree, Book Bank.
I'm Looking for My Hat, Arthur Speer, Book Bank.
In the Park, John McInnes and John Ryckman, Early Bird.
What Shall I Wear?, Pauline Cartwright, Scholastic.

Books That Draw Attention to the Print

Chew, Chew, Chew, Lucy Lawrence. Literacy 2000.
Dark Night, Sleepy Night, Harriet Ziefert, Scholastic.
The Dippy Dinner Drippers, Joy Cowley, Sunshine.
Follow That Fish, Joanne Oppenheim, Bank Street.
Grandpa Snored, Susan King, Literacy 2000.
The Jacket I Wear in the Snow, Shirley Neitzel, Scholastic.
Let's Go to Sally's Place, Pat Edwards, Eureka.
The Smallest Turtle, Lynley Dodd, Early Bird.
Sssh!, Jan McPherson, Book Bank.
Wizard McBean and His Flying Machine, Dennis Nolan, Prentice-Hall.
Woosh!, June Melser and Joy Cowley, Story Box.

Professional Books and Articles

Must Reads

Bialostock, S. (1992). *Raising Readers.* Winnipeg, MB: Peguis.

Provides parents with specific information about what to look for as their child's reading develops, and how to support that development.

Clay, M. (1991). *Becoming literate: The Construction of Inner Control.* Portsmouth, NH: Heinemann.

Discusses in depth how successful readers gain gradual control over reading and writing and points out the implications for working with children who experience difficulties.

DeFord, D., Lyons, C., and Pinnell, G. (1993). *Bridges to Literacy: Learning from Reading Recovery.* Portsmouth, NH: Heinemann.
Contains a collection of articles focusing the relationship between one-to-one instruction and classroom instruction.

Doake, D. (1988). *Reading Begins at Birth.* Richmond Hill, ON: Scholastic.
A very readable description of natural reading development.

Holdaway, D. (1979). *The Foundations of Literacy.* Sydney: Ashton Scholastic.
A seminal book about literacy learning.

Holdaway, D. (1980). *Independence in Reading.* 2d edition. Sydney: Ashton Scholastic.
Discusses individualized teaching strategies. Of particular interest is the section on basic sight words in context.

Kemp, M. (1987). *Watching Children Read and Write: Observational Records for Children with Special Needs.* Portsmouth, NH: Heinemann.
An excellent collection of procedures and reproducible recording sheets for assessing literacy development. Offers alternatives to standardized assessment.

Phinney, M. (1988). *Reading with the Troubled Reader.* Richmond Hill, ON: Scholastic Canada, and Portsmouth, NH: Heinemann.
A must read. Describes children with reading difficulties and ways to assist them.

Rhodes, L., and Dudley-Marling, C. (1988). *Readers and Writers with a Difference: A Holistic Approach to Teaching Learning Disabled and Remedial Students.* Portsmouth, NH: Heinemann.
Considers holistic reading and writing instruction as it relates to learning disabled and remedial students, along with appropriate instructional strategies.

Smith, F. (1978). *Reading Without Nonsense.* New York: Teacher's College Press.
An insightful look at the process of learning to read and how schools can most effectively support an individual's attempt to join the literacy club.

Stires, S. (ed.) (1991). *With Promise: Redefining Reading and Writing for "Special Students."* Portsmouth, NH: Heinemann.
A look at creating positive environments for students in need of support.

Watson, A., and Badenhop, A. (eds.) (1992). *Prevention of Reading Failure.* Sydney: Ashton Scholastic.
A broad overview of the issues in the teaching of reading, with an interesting chapter on phonemic awareness.

Practical Titles

Bookshelf Teacher's Resource Book. (1986). Sydney: Ashton Scholastic.

Baskwill, J. (1989). *Parents and Teachers: Partners in Learning.* Richmond Hill, ON: Scholastic Canada.

Baskwill, J., and Baskwill, S. (1991). *Language Arts Sourcebook: Scholastic sourcebook for Grades 5 & 6.* Richmond Hill, ON: Scholastic Canada.

Baskwill, J., and Whitman, P. (1986). *Whole Language Sourcebook.* Richmond Hill, ON: Scholastic Canada.

Baskwill, J., and Whitman, P. (1988). *Evaluation: Whole Language, Whole Child.* Richmond Hill, ON: Scholastic Canada.

Baskwill, J., and Whitman, P. (1988). *Moving On: Scholastic Sourcebook for Grades 3 & 4.* Richmond Hill, ON: Scholastic Canada.

Booth, D., Booth, J., and Phenix, J. (1994). *Assessment and Evaluation.* Toronto, ON: MeadowBook Press.

Clay, M. (1982). *Observing Young Readers.* Auckland, NZ: Heinemann.

Clay, M. (1982). *SAND, A Diagnostic Survey: Concepts about Print Test.* Auckland, NZ: Heinemann.

Goodman, Y., and Burke, C. (1972). *Reading Miscue Inventory Manual: Procedures for Diagnosis and Evaluation.* New York: Macmillan.

Rhodes, L. (1993). *Literacy Assessment: A Handbook of Instruments.* Portsmouth, NH: Heinemann.